UNLIMITED MEMORY

HOW TO USE ADVANCED LEARNING STRATEGIES TO LEARN FASTER, REMEMBER MORE AND BE MORE PRODUCTIVE

GRANDMASTER KEVIN HORSLEY

ISBN: 978-1-63161-998-4

Published by TCK Publishing

www.TCKPublishing.com

DEDICATION

This book is dedicated to Eloise Cooper. I would like to acknowledge the contributions that you made to this book and thank you so much for all your encouragement and support in my life.

CONTENTS

"Memory is a way of holding onto the things you love, the things you are, the things you never want to lose."

~ The Wonder Years

FOREWORD

With this book, Kevin brings to life principles that can change your life forever. I say this with confidence because I have studied and implemented these methods in my own life. There are so many areas in your life and existence that can be transformed by these principles that I am honored to make such a small contribution to this amazing body of work.

While studying to be a medical doctor, I didn't know these methods and in academic performance I was an average medical student. I would spend many an hour battling through random bits of information while struggling to make sense of it. The question is not whether I made it or not but rather how much more efficient I could have been while working towards my qualification. The first time I encountered Kevin's methods was while training to be a medical specialist. It has completely changed the way I now approach studying and how I now manage information – with a straight "A" academic record as added benefit. With this bit of information I sincerely complement the author of this book. I did not suddenly change into some 'intelligent being'; I decided to transform my perceptions about my memory. With this new-found structure and purpose, I managed to discover a potential within myself that I never thought possible.

After realizing the impact of these principles in my academic life, I started applying it to my everyday life. What a journey this has been! The experience has been so much more than just learning to manage information; it ultimately enhanced my self-confidence, and the consequence of this cannot be limited to a specific area of my life.

I am privileged to know Kevin personally and seeing the information written in this book evident in his life has been such a great source of motivation for me!

After many years of research, experience, and achievement, Kevin shares life-changing methods with us in an easy-to-understand and practical way. When you decide to utilize these methods and make them your own, you will unleash unlimited potential to not only improve your memory, but your life as well.

~ Dr Marius A. Welgemoed

CHAPTER 1

INTRODUCTION

"The great breakthrough in your life comes when you realize that you can learn anything you need to learn to accomplish any goal that you set for yourself. This means there are no limits on what you can be, have or do."

~ Brian Tracy

What would your life be like if you could learn and remember information easily, quickly, and effectively? Think about it.

In this short, easy-to-read book I will provide you with a set of powerful memory-enhancing mindsets and skills, which will allow you to take control of your learning and your life. You will discover many amazing methods, both ancient and new, that have been modeled from the world's best minds in the areas of accelerated learning and memory development. This book will give you information that school forgot to teach you. The approach is all about running your own brain; I believe that this can only be possible with the foundation of memory.

Imagine if you were born without a memory. Who would you be? You would be nothing; if you don't have a memory, you don't have anything else. If I ask you, "Who are you?" you would immediately start rearranging memories in your mind to answer that question. Your memory is the glue that binds your life together; everything you are today is because of your amazing memory. You are a data collecting being, and your memory is where your life is lived. If you didn't have a memory, you wouldn't be able to learn, think, have intelligence, create, or even know how to tie your shoes. You wouldn't be able to build experience in any field because experience is just a collection of memories after all! **Only if you can remember information can you live it.**

Over the years, memory has been given a bad name. It has been associated with rote learning and cramming information into your brain. Educators have said that understanding is the key to learning but how can you understand something if you can't remember it? We have all had this experience: we recognize and understand information but can't recall it when we need it. For example, how many jokes do you know?

You've probably heard thousands, but you can only recall about four or five right now. There is a big difference between remembering your four jokes and recognizing or understanding thousands. Understanding doesn't create use: only when you can instantly recall what you understand, and practise using your remembered understanding, do you achieve mastery. Memory means storing what you have learned; otherwise, why would we bother learning in the first place?

Some people say you don't need a good memory in the Google age. Ken Jennings said, *"When you make a decision, you need facts. If those facts are in your brain, they're at your fingertips. If they're all in Google somewhere, you may not make the right decision on the spur of the moment."*

Which raises the question: would or have you hired a person for his or her ability to Google information? No, you want people with information and experience at their fingertips. You want confident people, people that are certain about what they know. Not storing information in your mind is expensive and can lead to embarrassment and poor judgment. If you have to continually refer to notes or manuals to do your work, you will waste time and look unprofessional. Would you rather buy a product from someone that forgets your name or from someone that remembers it? Would you allow a doctor to operate on you if she had to continually refer to a manual or an iPad? Definitely not!

Memory is the corner stone of our existence. It determines the quality of our decisions and, therefore, our entire life!

Learning and memory are the two most magical properties of the human mind. Learning is the ability to acquire new information, and memory holds the new information in place over time. Memory is the foundation to all learning. If memory is not set in place, all you are doing is throwing information into a deep hole never to be used again. The problem is that many people are not recalling what they know, and they are constantly learning and forgetting, and learning and forgetting, and learning and forgetting...

When you improve your memory, you improve everything. You can access information more quickly and more easily – creating greater opportunities for connections and associations. The more facts and memories that you have properly stored in your brain, the more potential you have to make unique combinations and connections. An increased memory also enhances basic intelligence because intelligence is based on all of the events, people, and facts that you can recall. The more you remember, the more you can create and do because factual knowledge always precedes skill. Information can only be built onto more information, so the more you know the easier it is to get to know more.

Now, with your memory you have two choices. The first choice is that your memory cannot be improved;

you can do nothing to make any difference to your in-born ability. Many people choose this as their life's choice because through the thousands of hours of schooling, not one hour is spent on showing you how your amazing memory can be made better. School never told you anything about your amazing brain.

When I was eight years old, a school psychologist gave me a bit of advice about my brain. He said I may have a form of brain damage, and he wanted to send me to a special class. I was a classic dyslexic: I wasn't born with a good memory, and I couldn't concentrate; reading and writing were always a challenge for me. Throughout my school career, I learned by having my mother and friends read the syllabus to me; I forced myself to memorize it and what I didn't get, which was most of it, I just didn't get. I had no future because I just couldn't grasp what was being taught to me. In twelve years of school, I couldn't read a book from cover-to-cover alone and in my final year of school, I still couldn't read much better than when I started out in First Grade. To cut a long story short, I somehow managed to graduate from high school in 1989.

A couple of years later, my life was changed when I was walking through a local bookstore. Up until that point, I had not read a book from cover-to-cover by myself, but that night I decided to buy three books. They were all written by Tony Buzan. The first book was *Use Your Head*, the second *Use Your Memory*, and the third *The Speed Reading Book*. Back then, I honestly thought I would begin with the speed reading book and then read the other two quickly. However, it didn't work out that way. I started reading *Use Your Memory* and discovered that we all have a second choice. This choice is: our memory is just a habit, and habits can be improved with the right kind of training and practice. I discovered that there are basic fundamentals to memory improvement and that if we apply them consistently, we will get the same results that great memory masters do. If we don't, we won't.

I started studying psychology and anything I could get my hands on in the areas of the brain, mind, and memory. I studied hundreds of books and tapes, and I also interviewed people with great memories. Through this long journey, I overcame all of my dyslexic issues and took myself to a point where I was reading and taking in, on average, four books a week. I could learn in an hour what took the average person months to master.

In 1995, I decided to compete in the World Memory Championships. This is an event that attracts the best memory masters from around the world, and the competition tests every facet of memory. That year I managed to come fifth overall, having won second place in the written word event. This was proof that I had overcome all of my dyslexic challenges. I was also awarded the title 'International Grandmaster of Memory' by the Brain Trust: a title, which was presented and jointly sanctioned by His Serene

Highness Prince Philip of Liechtenstein, on October 26th, 1995 at Hanbury Manor in Ware, Hertfordshire, England. Considering my past difficulties and from where I had come, this was a great achievement. From that day on, I knew my life had changed direction, and it would never be the same again.

In 1999, I decided to stretch myself and test my abilities even more when I broke the world record that has been called 'The Everest of Memory Tests.' I memorized the first 10,000 digits of Pi – Pi has passed every test of randomness and has no known limit. The first 10,000 digits of Pi are divided into 2000 5-digit groups. The testers would randomly call out any one of these 5-digit sequences, and I had to reply with the 5-digit numbers on either side of the number chosen. This happened 50 times. The record was for the time taken to complete the test; I broke the previous record by 14 minutes. Why did I do it, you ask? Mainly because people said it was impossible to do, and that's what my life is all about: breaking limitations and showing people what our memories are capable of.

Ever since then, I have been training, teaching, and coaching people to remember key information that they need for their lives and that the joy of learning is available to us all. Many people say I have a photographic memory, but that is not true. I have just discovered many 'secrets' about memory, and I have been able to use and make these methods my own.

I don't tell you all this to impress you but to impress the point that every person has the same potential to master his or her memory. It doesn't matter where you come from; all that matters is where you are going. However, if you keep on doing what you have always done, you are going to get what you have always gotten. You need to *do* different to *get* different. Thus, a word of warning: **mastering your memory is going to require a different kind of thinking.**

Don't judge or look for perfection from this book; rather look for value. When you judge information, you stop yourself from learning it. You can judge the methods, you can criticize them, you can try another approach, but I promise you, you will not be able to get the same results as us memory masters without applying these principles. I ask you to read with an open mind; I have no doubt that everything that you will learn in this book works and works amazingly well. The methods that I will share with you are the same methods that memory masters use. This is the strategy!

You will see that this book is broken up into three sections covering the four keys (or Cs) to improving your memory. The first section talks about improving your Concentration. The second section is about improving your ability to Create imagery and Connecting concepts together, and the final key is about creating a habit with Continuous use. These four Cs are the solution to any memory problem that you have or will face in the future. Some of the examples that I have used in this book come from personal development and business books so not only will you learn to improve your memory, but you will also learn some key concepts that you can use for your personal development.

I will teach you to transform bland information into something that is real and well organized. This, in turn, means the information has meaning and will then be used instead of being discarded. I am not talking about rote learning but a way to store information differently with far better results. The goal is to improve learning and understanding.

There are many books out there that do a lot of talking before you find any meat. This book is different; I want to get straight to the point and save you a lot of time and energy. It is my goal to show you the wonderful world of memory improvement in a way I wish someone would have taught me. Don't just read this book; play with the concepts and make it part of your thinking and your life. If you are ready, then turn to the first lesson and unleash the power of your memory.

PART 1

CONCENTRATE

"The best advice I ever came across on the subject of concentration is: Wherever you are, be there."

~ Jim Rohn

CHAPTER 2

EXCUSE ME

"You cannot fly with the eagles if you
continue to scratch with the turkeys."

~ Zig Ziglar

Before we begin, what excuses are you going to make for not reading this whole book?

If you decide to read the whole book, what excuses are you going to make for not using the information that you are going to learn? I know you don't know what you will be learning, but you have those excuses all lined up, don't you? Take time to really think about your excuses and write them down.

These are the same excuses that you use every time to stop yourself from learning anything new. You can have success or excuses, but you can't have them both. People that learn quickly only focus on the information and skills that matter – excuses don't matter, and they are thought viruses.

The only things that are keeping you from getting what you want in your life are the excuses you keep telling yourself. Who would you be without your excuses? Think about it.

Every excuse you accept makes you weaker. Excuses stop you from concentrating and paying attention. When you excuse yourself from learning something new, you block your focus and your energy. Always remember that **where your attention goes, your energy flows**.

Some of the most common excuses that people use to give away their power are:

1. I AM HELPLESS

I'm not smart enough.

It's not my nature.

I don't have the time to practise the information (Time is always there; you just need to schedule it.)

I don't have the right genes to have a good memory (How do you really know that?)

I am getting older; I can't do anything about my memory.

You can't teach old dogs new tricks! (Then it is a good thing you are not a dog!)

2. Someone Else Is To Blame

My parents always said that I was stupid.

I need support to develop these skills.

It is the book's fault; I need to experience it in a seminar.

It is impossible to have a negative emotion without blaming someone or something. Free your mind. You always have two choices with your life and experience: you can either learn from it or you can place blame. The choice is always yours.

3. Too Much Stress

There is just too much to learn.

I have to change my thinking.

The book requires me to do too much.

It will be difficult.

We excuse ourselves into living mediocre lives. We explain why we can't do this or that; we excuse ourselves from taking responsibility. Decide now to stop giving away your power to your excuses.

Are your excuses true? Are you 100% certain that they are true? Do any of your excuses really enhance and empower your life? You are more than your excuses, aren't you?

Drop them now!

Richard Bach said, *"Argue for your limitations and, sure enough, they're yours."* The only cause for not doing something with the information in this book is you; nobody else but you. You are responsible for your learning. The person that has the most to do with what happens to you is you! **If you believe your limits, your life will be very limited.**

Improving your memory and concentration is not only about what you need to do more of; it is also about what you need to do less of. It is amazing how quickly you can learn a new skill when you decide to let go of your excuses, judgments, and complaints. If you consistently change your approach and increase your desire to learn this information, you will master it.

Take Action Now!

1. If you continue to hold on to your excuses, what would your life be like five years from now?
2. Who would you be without your excuses? Enter all learning with this new mindset.
3. Remember they are just excuses. It is not the truth. Change them now.
4. What is more important to you: excusing yourself from experiencing your potential or being the best that you can be?
5. Why is it important for you to learn to empower your memory? Think about it and write down as many reasons as you can to create a big WHY. As

Darren Hardy says, *"We need why power not willpower."*

Why do you want to improve your memory?

- learning new languages will be more efficient
- Better overall Job performance
- Remembering names
- More RAM to all endeavors
- Recall books better
- overall life additions

CHAPTER 3

NEVER BELIEVE A LIE

"The mind is the limit. As long as the mind can envision the fact that you can do something, you can do it – as long as you believe 100 percent."

~ Arnold Schwarzenegger

There was once a fish that lived in a pond. One day, he met another fish that used to live in the sea. The pond fish asked, "What is the sea?" and the sea fish said, "It is a vast amount of water that is a million, million times bigger than your pond." The pond fish never talked to the sea fish again because he thought the sea fish was a liar.

What can we learn from this?

Your beliefs of what your concentration and memory can do may be your own limited version of the truth. Many people never get a taste of their true potential because they have decided to entertain only a limited view of what they can do.

What if your negative beliefs about your concentration, your memory, and your potential were not true at all? Who would you be without these beliefs?

Richard Bandler said,

"Beliefs aren't about truth. Beliefs are about believing. They are guides for our behavior."

We always defend what we believe. If you believe you have a bad memory, you will always act and think in accordance with that belief. Where your attention goes, your energy flows.

If you want to improve your memory and concentration, you need to create a belief system that supports them.

Imagine there is an **Earth 1** and an **Earth 2**. The planets are the same in every way, but... they are in different dimensions.

On **Earth 1** lives **Mr. A** and on **Earth 2** lives **Mr. B**.

They look the same, they speak the same way, they live in the same environment, they have the same education, and they even have the same brain and nervous system. Everything is the same. There is only one thing that separates them.

Mr. A believes that he has a terrible memory. He always tells people:

"My attention is all over the place; it is like a kangaroo hopping around my mind."

"I'm always forgetting things."

"I'm terrible with names."

"My memory is getting worse every day."

"My memory is full."

"My memory is like a sieve."

"I'm stupid."

"Your brain will fill up – so don't learn too much!"

He hates learning. He is not interested in remembering because he thinks he will forget.

Mr. B believes he has a wonderful memory; in fact, an exceptional memory. He always says:

"I choose to focus my attention; it is like a laser beam."

"Memory improvement is important."

"Look how much I remember: I have quadrillions of memories stored in my mind."

"My memory is getting better and better every day."

"I'm interested in remembering names."

"I'm brilliant."

"My memory has the ability to store and recall mountains of information. It is the only container with this characteristic: the more I put into it, the more it will hold."

He loves learning. He wants to remember and train his mind.

Now, who do you think will have the better memory? Of course: **Mr. B**.

The only difference between **Mr. A** and **Mr. B** is their beliefs. Whose beliefs do you think are right?

The answer is that they are both right. It is only our thinking that makes things right or wrong. **Mr. A** and **Mr. B** both have beliefs, and they both have experiences or thoughts to back it up. The only difference is that **Mr. A's** focus is negative and disempowering. He sets himself up to fail.

Mr. B's focus is positive and empowering. He sets himself up for success. Both **Mr. A** and **Mr. B** choose their own beliefs. It isn't an outside influence that determines their outcome. We all have the freedom to choose what we focus on and in the end, it will determine the beliefs we carry around with us.

A belief is a sense of being certain and what you believe, you become.

Negative beliefs and thoughts place a block on your concentration and memory. Unless you decide to take responsibility and change the thoughts that you are constantly feeding yourself, you will not be able to break through your negative conditioning. Every single thought we have is creative: it has the power to build and the power to destroy.

Most people don't realize that when they use doubtful phrases they are setting standards for themselves. These standards become expectations and in the end will become self-fulfilling prophecies.

Overleaf is an example of what happens with a negative belief frame:

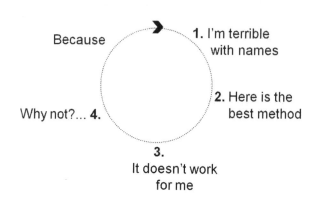

Because

1. I'm terrible
with names

Why not?... **4.**

2. Here is the
best method

3.
It doesn't work
for me

Your limiting belief will keep you trapped in a loop.
Your mind will keep looping and prevent you from
learning anything new. Your beliefs either move you or
stop you. In brief, every thought and every word works
for you or against you, and every thought that you
confirm to be true multiplies and becomes a belief.
When you change a belief you change a mental
construction and, therefore, your life. In other words,
we believe what we have been taught to believe, and
we don't question beliefs because we don't want to
question the source. Begin to ask yourself, "Who will I
be doubting by changing my beliefs about my mind,
concentration, and memory and why do I think this is
true?"

People tend to think that their beliefs are absolutely
true, but these beliefs are only true for them. Just
because you can't do something well doesn't mean it is
impossible. Identify your self-limiting beliefs and then
ask, "What if they were not true at all?" and remember

The first step is 24 to empower your
Mind and believe

the limits in your belief system will always stop you from seeing any alternatives that should be obvious.

If you choose to change your beliefs, here is how you can do it:

First, 80% of changing anything is about **why** you want to change and only 20% is about **how** you do it. Take responsibility; it is as simple as having a reason and making a decision that you want to change your beliefs.

Second, question the belief. There are some things that you previously believed with all your heart but now you don't believe them. Why? Because you questioned them. If, long ago, some teacher told you that you have a memory like a sieve, it doesn't mean you have to make the teacher's words true or a reality. You were younger then, had less experience, and did not have the ability to question authority. Now with age comes the advantage that you can question his or her judgment of your younger self. Ask yourself questions like, "How much is this belief going to cost me if I hold on to it? Do I have to hold on to it? Is it true? Can I be 100% certain that it is the truth?"

Third, create a new belief and think of experiences, research, and thoughts to confirm it. When you change your beliefs, you allow yourself to experience more of your potential and create new possibilities.

Fourth, use the new belief often and make it part of your identity.

Your beliefs are only the stories that you have accepted to be true about yourself... just decide to change the stories.

Spenser Lord said, *"Beliefs are not tattoos, they are just like clothes – you can put them on and take them off at will."* Thus, here are **five core beliefs that you can 'put on' right now**:

1. I WAS BORN WITH EXCEPTIONAL CONCENTRATION AND MEMORY

You are already all you need to be. Maxwell Maltz said, *"Do not tolerate for a minute the idea that you are prohibited from any achievement by the absence of inborn talent or ability. This is a lie of the grandest order, an excuse of the saddest kind."* You don't need anything more. You don't need a special talent or pill to have brilliant concentration or a great memory. All you need is a willingness to learn, a method, and self-discipline.

2. MEMORY IMPROVEMENT IS IMPORTANT

Successful people believe that what they do is important and worth doing. With this belief, people move from interest into commitment. **Consider living without your memory for one week. You wouldn't be capable of doing anything.** Everything you do, say, and understand is due to memory. It is your most important mental function and if you improve it, you will improve your life.

3. I HAVE INCREDIBLE ABILITIES. MY MEMORY IS UNLIMITED

Think about how much data you already have stored in your memory (numbers, stories, jokes, experiences, words, names, and places.) Think about what an incredible memory you need just to have a conversation. You have to listen, create meaning from what you have just heard, and then search your memory for a response. **Not even all the computers in existence connected to each other can perform such a feat.** You will see your incredible ability once you have learned the memory methods.

4. THERE IS NO FAILURE, ONLY FEEDBACK

Catch your memory doing things right. One of the best ways to strengthen this belief is to ask yourself, "How does my memory serve me – how did it serve me today?" Generally, people only focus on where their memory went wrong; therefore, making it weaker. Focus on your strengths and change your approach when the feedback or result is not what you want.

5. I DON'T KNOW IT ALL

Thinking you know everything there is to know about something is really not a useful place to be because it prevents you from learning anything new. Listen and become interested in other points of view and embrace change as well as new things. Allow information to come to you. Open all channels to receive information.

Decide now that you will only feed your mind with good. Adopt and try on as many empowering beliefs as you can. Use them and watch your life take on a new direction.

TAKE ACTION NOW!

1. Identify your self-limiting beliefs.

2. Question these beliefs and ask yourself: "Is it I **can't** improve my concentration and memory or is it I **won't** make the time to improve my concentration and memory?"

3. What else do you believe about your mind and your potential?

4. Memorize this quote by Jim Rohn, *"If you don't like how things are, change it! You're not a tree."*

CHAPTER 4

BE HERE NOW

"Concentrate all your thoughts on the task at hand. The sun's rays do not burn until brought to a focus."

~ Alexander Graham Bell

We are all gifted: gifted with the power to think about our thinking. You can focus your thinking to improve any area of your life; you are in control of what you choose to attend to. You can continue to allow your attention to be pulled by your environment, or you can decide now to direct it.

Many people believe super concentration is a magical state with which only a lucky few are born. For instance, do you agree with this statement: big muscular biceps are something you are born with? No of course not because we all know it takes many hours of training in a gym. Yet, people look at attention as something you have or don't have. Concentration, like anything in life, takes practice.

Concentration is made up of many small choices consistently practised. Everyday brain research is telling us that the brain is consistently changing when we learn something new. The people that limit their attention are still using the 'your-brain-can't-change' model. We know that concentration can and should be improved. You have everything in you now to take control of your bouncing monkey mind and to take your power back.

Here is the average person's daily attention training: they wake up in the morning, not peacefully, usually to some loud song or blaring alarm clock. They check their mobile phone for any messages, just to see if anyone missed them. Then they jump out of bed into the shower and there they think about a hundred and ten things that they need to worry about or need to do. Unfortunately, they haven't allowed themselves enough time to get ready and can only manage a small unhealthy breakfast and fill up with coffee. They get in their car, put the radio on, make phone calls, or even try to text messages in the traffic. They get all angry, and they get all worked up about the traffic. The traffic is there and won't change; yet, they think it should change. In fact, we worry and focus our attention on a 'million' things which can all wait for the appropriate time, but we allow our attention to be pulled in different directions.

Imagine your attention was an Olympic athlete. Would your athlete be able to be competitive? The reason our attention and focus isn't that great is because we haven't trained it. We keep on switching through the channels of our minds and never stop long enough on one specific channel. We pay attention half-heartedly on almost everything we do these days. We live in an activity illusion and think that 'busyness' is equal to good business. Busyness is sometimes just procrastination in disguise. Busyness may make you feel good and make you think you are more productive but when we look back at the end of the day we realize we haven't done anything worthwhile. We are training our minds to have continuous partial attention, and our attention is being fragmented.

Training your concentration isn't that hard. You just have to learn to become more peaceful and find the moment. You have to learn to be here now. When you are at work, be at work. When you are at home, be at home. *"Learn to be silent. Let your quiet mind listen and absorb,"* said Pythagoras.

We fill our minds up with all kinds of conflict, and this takes us away from the moment. Have you ever had a fight with someone at home, then you get to work, and the whole day you can't concentrate? Conflict pulls your mind in many directions; when you fill your mind with conflict, your mind will be all over the place. **Conflict is the opposite of concentration.**

When you are peaceful, you enjoy the moment and your mind becomes like a laser beam. Peace and concentration are the same thing.

There are four areas that you need to focus on to eliminate conflict and create more peace in your mind:

1. TAKE CONTROL OF YOUR INNER VOICE

Do you have a little voice that talks to you in your head? If you are not sure, you are probably asking yourself, "Do I have a little voice or don't I?" We all have a little voice, and it has a huge influence on our concentration and our lives. You are constantly talking to yourself but the only problem is that you catch yourself doing things wrong. **Start to catch yourself doing more things right.**

How or where did you concentrate well today? In what area of your life do you need to stop 'beating' yourself up?

Your inner voice has the ability to offer instructions so instruct yourself well. It is the center of your focus of control that helps you explain and make sense of your world. Don't agree with the wrong voices; all self-hatred and conflict is just a thought or a little voice... so change the thought. It is not set in stone. Remember: if you give yourself bad commands, then bad things will happen.

2. STOP MULTITASKING

We destroy our concentration by multitasking the moment and our peace away. Multitasking is a myth!

If you watch a lioness hunting in the wild, she will focus on one wildebeest. She never focuses on two – because she knows the odds of missing both are stacked against her. She is single minded and does everything in her power to achieve her goal. In the circus when they train lions, they put a chair in front of their face to control their behavior. This confuses the lion and divides their attention. Now they have four chair legs to focus on, and they go into a type of trance. We humans are the same. Our brain can really only focus on one thing at a time. It is impossible to focus on two things at the same time. When you are multitasking, you are actually switching between tasks, you are always semi-attending, and it is not very effective. We cannot do more than one thing well at a time. It has become one of the most damaging myths out there.

We are training our brains to have an attention deficit. A lot of people simply cannot focus for an extended period of time anymore. I have heard that the average person looks at their mobile phone about 50 times a day. We are reading emails, the news, Facebook, and Twitter etc., during what should be family and relationship time. People these days even drive while talking on a phone. Driving with a mobile phone makes you hit the brakes 0.5 seconds slower. If you are travelling at 112km per hour, in 0.5seconds you travel 15.5 meters... a lot can happen over that distance. If you are distracted in your car, you have a 9 times higher chance of having an accident. When your phone rings, you don't have to pick it up... that's why voice mail was invented!

Neuroscience consultant Marilee Springer says, *"Multi-tasking is known to slow people down by 50% and add 50% more mistakes."* Multi-tasking is like putting your brain on drugs. There is a whole body of research that shows that multitasking is less productive, makes you less creative, and contributes to you making bad decisions.

We are also not allowing ourselves to sit and enjoy the moment anymore. Blaise Pascal said, *"All man's miseries derive from not being able to sit quietly in a room alone."* We get in the car, and we **have to** put the radio on. When we arrive home we **have to** put the TV on. When we watch TV, we flip through the channels. We even lack enough attention to watch the commercials. We are constantly filling our minds with conflict. Most people allow their attention to be pulled in different directions; very few people direct their attention. A lack of **attention direction** is the real disorder.

Stop overwhelming yourself by continually changing the channels of your mind. Sharpen up your intellect by returning to the habit of doing one thing at a time. Rediscover the value of consecutive tasking, instead of settling for the quality dilution associated with simultaneous tasking. Exceptional work is always associated with periods of deep concentration. Nothing excellent ever comes from a scattered effort. When you are all there, your brain power and resources will be all there, too.

3. KNOW WHAT YOU WANT

When people approach information they never really know what they want out of it. They don't direct their minds. Learn to engage and be present with information by creating a strong **PIC** in your mind:

Purpose: Having a clear purpose is important because clarity dissolves resistance. Always remember why you are reading or learning the information. Keep your purpose at the forefront of your mind. If you don't know what you want, how are you going to know when you get it? Learning with a purpose increases your attention, comprehension, retention, and organizes your thoughts. The more specific the purpose, the more information you will get. A vague purpose would be: I want to learn more about memory from this book. A specific purpose would be: I want to learn at least six key strategies that will enable me to improve my memory. Focus on getting information that you can use – and then put it into practice. As David Allen said, "If you're not sure why you're doing something, you can never do enough of it."

Interest: Your level of interest sets the direction of your attention and, therefore, your level of focus. If you are not interested, remembering what you read will be almost impossible. Whatever is highest on your interest list is where your mind is alert, disciplined, and focused. Whatever is lower on your interest list is where you hesitate and procrastinate.

You can remember mountains of information when you are interested in the subject. It almost feels automatic and your concentration is at a peak. Your deficits of attention are mostly interest deficits. **Your mind never wanders away; it only moves towards more interesting and outstanding things.**

We all know that interest improves concentration but how do we get interested in the 'boring' information? The first step is to find your interests and then to find links or connections between your interests and the new information that you are learning. For example, I'm interested in training and sharing knowledge with other people. When I read anything I'm always searching for new information relating to my interest. When I read or listen through my interest filter, I am focused and I can concentrate. I always ask myself questions like, "How does this connect to training? How is it going to improve my life? If I read or remember this, is it going to give me something that not many people know? Is it going to help me in the future? How does this material help me achieve my goals?" In other words, all 'boring' information can be made more interesting with the right mindset. Gilbert Chesterton said, *"There are no uninteresting things, only uninterested people."* **So get interested!**

Curiosity: Questions are the answer to improving curiosity. Before you start reading or learning anything, ask yourself motivational questions. Most people ask questions that don't move them to take action. They look at the book and say things like, "Why do I have to read this book? This is too much to read. This looks really boring." If you ask questions like that, how much energy are you going to have to learn? You want to ask energy enhancing questions that get you engaged in the information. Ask yourself, "How is this relevant and applicable to my life right now? How will this information help me achieve my goals? How can I apply this information to improve my work? How will this help me? How will this information make me more significant?" Get curious about your mind and how it works. Tony Robbins says, *"If you want to cure boredom, be curious. If you're curious, nothing is a chore; it's automatic – you want to study. Cultivate curiosity, and life becomes an unending study of joy."*

4. ELIMINATE WORRY

Imagine one day you woke up and you didn't **have to** worry. What would you feel like? You would be peaceful; there would be no thoughts moving through your mind. No thoughts sending stress emotions through your system.

Imagine waking up and you didn't **have to** run or control other people's behaviors or control the government with your thinking. Imagine you didn't have to believe the latest fear rumor.

Byron Katie says, *"I could only find three kinds of business in the world - mine, yours, and God's. Whose business are you in?"* You become more relaxed when you decide to take up residence in your own mind and your own business. Life is easy when you simplify and make peace with your train of thought. When you believe your 'bad' thinking; you suffer. How many people, events, and things did you try to control with your mind today? Stay in your own mind and enjoy the laser like energy of having a clear mind.

You don't worry because you care; you worry because that is what you have learned to do. Worry is a very creative mental process. The questions you ask in your mind create your worries. If you ask 'what if' questions, you set your mind up to worry. If you consistently ask, "What if I lose my job? What if I crash my car? What if criminals attack me?" All these 'what if' phrases create 'movies' in your mind that constantly loop different scenarios, which creates a state of worry. Rather, say to yourself, "**What would I do** if I lost my job? What would I do if I crashed my car?" These movies that are created by these questions don't loop you into worry. They give you action steps that direct your mind. Create a procedure for different scenarios and make peace with your thinking.

Learn to practise peace because if you have no attention you have no retention.

Most people swing from one emotional extreme to the other. Concentration is about learning how to stay centered. When you concentrate your power, you can achieve anything. Imagine your mind was a torch. Most people allow their torch to jump and shine all over the place. You want your torch to stand still and shine brightly. Nothing outside of you is going to fix your concentration; it is an inside job.

You need to make a decision today: do you want to improve your concentration or don't you? It is always up to you. Therefore, eliminate your excuses, clean up your beliefs, and be here now!

Change thinking from "What if" → "What would I do?"

PART 2

CREATE AND CONNECT

"When you train your creativity, you automatically train your memory. When you train your memory, you automatically train your creative thinking skills!"

~ Tony Buzan

CHAPTER 5

BRING INFORMATION TO LIFE

"Your mind is the greatest home entertainment centre ever created."

~ Mark Victor Hansen

Many people dream of having a photographic memory. They define it as the ability to take a quick mental picture of information (without effort), and then describe it in detail from memory. In this case, your mind would be like a camera taking photos of anything you need to know. Unfortunately, all perfect memory takes some conscious effort and photographic memory is a myth.

Memory is a creative process and not a photographic process. Many people who are thought to have a photographic memory are just using all the methods that you will learn in this book on some or other level.

If you take these methods into your life you will be tapping into your natural memory power too. Perfect memory is a skill and not some special gift.

Have you ever had this experience? You are in an exam, and you know exactly what page the information is on but you don't know what is on the page. Or, you are reading something and you get to the bottom of the page and you think to yourself, "What have I just read?" The reason this happens is because you never brought the information to life.

Think about it... what happens when you read a novel or a story? You make a kind of movie in your mind, don't you? You can remember all the names of the characters, places, and events because you can see it and you are creating pictures all the time while reading. You are using your imagination and your natural creative ability.

However, when people start to learn textbook material they try to make a mental photograph or recording of the page but leave their creative abilities out of the learning process. People that learn quickly or have a so-called photographic memory apply their creativity to everything they learn. They may have either learned how to do this in the past or they have been using the principles naturally and unconsciously.

Most people try to remember information with their sense of sound. They repeat the information over and over again, hoping it will somehow stick. Sound is very limited because it doesn't attach easily to other memories. A sound is also always sequential; if you want to remember something with sound you have to start at the beginning and work your way through the information. However, when you see information as an image in your mind you can jump in and out of the information, and therefore improve your understanding too.

Any book that you really enjoy normally activates your imagination and brings the information to life. You naturally get engaged in the book and you battle to put it down because you don't want to turn the 'movie' off.

Your mind is like an internal movie screen on which you can ask it to produce information. This is how we think and learn effectively. Your brain creates miracles everyday by converting lifeless information into pictures and ideas. When you become aware of this, every word becomes a picture drawn with letters because words are only symbols of three-dimensional images. Arthur Gordon said, *"Isn't it amazing how we take them for granted? Those little black marks on paper. 26 different shapes known as letters, arranged in endless combinations, known as words, lifeless, until someone's eye falls on them."*

If your brain was unable to make images out of symbols, all learning and reading would be worthless and incredibly boring. Your brain likes pictures and we are really good at remembering them.

As neuroscientist John Medina says, *"Hear a piece of information and three days later you'll remember 10% of it. Add a picture and you'll remember 65%."*

Some people say, "I can't make pictures in my mind." We all make pictures in our mind. If you were unable to create or remember visual images, you would be severely handicapped. Learn to use your imagination; it is a learned skill and not a natural talent.

Reading and understanding is also a creative imagination process. It is a power that can be compared to magic. We succeed in this area when we produce images in our mind. When we don't, we feel confused or ignorant. If I tried to explain to you how a car engine works but you don't know what an engine looks like or if I didn't have one for you to look at or a drawing to represent it, it would be really difficult to understand.

The more we turn information into images or mind movies, the more we will remember and comprehend. We can learn to make all our learning more creative and memorable if we use our unlimited imagination.

You can learn to enhance your memory imagination system by making your mind movies exciting and sticky. The way to do this is with the '**SEE**' principle.

THE SEE PRINCIPLE

Use your **S – Senses**: there are only five ways to get anything into your brain, and that is through sight, sound, smell, touch, and taste. When you utilize your senses you experience more of life and you remember more.

Our senses help us mentally recreate our world. If you train your senses you will be using more of your brain, and if you learn to engage as many of your senses as you can then you will automatically improve your memory. Think of a horse: see it in your mind, touch it, smell it, hear it, and even taste it. You didn't see the letters H.O.R.S.E in your mind; you saw a multisensory picture of what the word represents. Your senses make mind movies real and memorable. Use them!

E – Exaggeration: what is easier to remember: a strawberry that is normal size or one the size of a house? Make your images larger or smaller than life. What is more memorable: an elephant or an elephant wearing a pink bikini?

Exaggerate with Humor; tickle your mind. **There is no scientific evidence to prove that learning should be serious.** Make your images illogical. Have fun; create some positive exaggerated learning memories.

E – Energize: give your pictures action. Would you rather watch a movie of your holiday or a slide show? What creates more feeling in your imagination: a horse standing still or a horse that is running and moving?

Make your information vivid, colorful, and not boring, flat and black and white. Use action; it brings life to your memories. Make your images act in illogical ways: you can weave, crash, stick, or wrap things together. We can make things talk, sing, and dance. Think about the great genius Walt Disney.

The process of imagination is a fun creative process. The more enjoyment you can put into it the better.

When you are reading, or hearing something, focus on all the SEE principles and imagine it is a movie. Even if you don't use a specific method that you will learn in this book, the SEE principles will improve your concentration. Emile Coue pointed out that, *"When the imagination and the will are in conflict, the imagination always wins."* If you 'will' yourself to remember, and your imagination is not on the task, you will have zero retention and recall. Your imagination is the place of all your memory power.

Some people say, "This is not the way that I naturally think."

This is not the way that I naturally think either; this is how I have taught myself to think, because it works. The more skilled you become in using your imagination the more you can know, comprehend, and create. In this way, you become the director of your own mind.

How do I turn abstract information into images?

We remember nouns and adjectives with ease because they have meaning and we can make a mental picture without much effort. Most abstract words can be made to mean something. Just use a meaningful thought or word to represent a 'meaningless' word. Find a word or phrase that sounds the same or similar to the abstract word, or you can break a word up into its individual sounds. Imagine you had to remember the name **Washington**; you could turn that word into a picture of you **washing** a **tin**. Or, if you had to remember the word **Hydrogen** you could see a picture of a fire **Hydrant** drinking **gin**.

You can turn all complex information into something meaningful and memorable by turning it into images. In the beginning it will take a bit of effort on your part. You will have to invest your attention at first and then it will become a habit. To practise look at words, break them up, make a picture and give it all more meaning. Let us learn a few foreign words for practice. Really imagine each word and create a SEE mini mind movie.

First, we will use **Spanish words**:

Tiger is **Tigre**, it sounds like tea grey. Imagine a *tiger* drinking his **tea** that has turned **grey**.

Sun is **Sole**. Imagine that the *sun* is burning the **sole** of your one foot.

Arm is **Brazo**. Imagine a **bra** is **sew**n onto your arm.

Some **Italian words**:

Chicken is **Polo**. You can imagine playing **polo** with a *chicken* instead of a ball.

Cat is **Gatto**. Imagine saying to your friend, "You've **got to** hold my *cat*."

Some **French words**:

Book is **Livre**. Sounds like liver, so you can imagine opening a *book* and finding squashed **liver** inside.

Hand is **Main**. My **main** hand is my right *hand*.

Chair is **Chez**. Imagine you have **shares** in a *chair*.

Some **Zulu words**:

Dog is **inja** (eenjaa). Think of an **injured** *dog*.

Floor is **phansi** (pansee). Imagine a **pansy** growing out of the *floor*.

Snake is **Inyoka** (eenyo'kaa). Imagine a *snake* slithering **in your car**.

Some **Japanese words**:

Chest is **Mune** (Mooneh). Imagine **money** growing out of your *chest*.

Door is **To** (Toe). Imagine you are kicking the *door* with your big **toe**.

Carpet is **Juutan** (Jootan). Imagine **you** are **tan**ning on a big *carpet*. Or, **you tan** a *carpet*.

Test yourself:

What is the Spanish word for tiger?

What is the Italian word for cat?

What is the Zulu word for dog?

What is the Japanese word for chest?

What is the French word for book?

What is the Italian word for chicken?

What is the Zulu word for snake?

What is the French word for hand?

What is the Japanese word for carpet?

Just by connecting these words in a silly mind movie you have learned fourteen foreign words. You can use this method to remember hundreds of foreign words if you use the SEE principle. Remember you are only connecting two concepts at a time. If you imagine it for a few seconds it will stick in your memory and it will be easy to recall if you need it.

You can even use this method to remember all the countries and capitals. You just need to bring the information to life.

The capital of **Australia** is **Canberra**, you can imagine a **Kangaroo** (represents Australia) eating a **can of berrie**s (Canberra) and the two will stick together making it more memorable.

The capital of **Greece** is **Athens**. Imagine **eight hens** (sounds like Athens) swimming in **Greece**.

The capital of **Madagascar** is **Antananarivo**. Imagine a **Mad gas car** crashing into your friend **Ann**, who is **tan**ning on **a river**.

The capital of **Belgium** is **Brussels**. Imagine Brussels sprouts falling out of a **bell** doing **gym** (Belgium.)

Make a silly picture and really SEE it and you can remember all the capitals with ease.

The greatest secret of a powerful memory is to bring information to life with your endless imagination. Take responsibility for your memory. You can only learn to control your memory when you become the source of your imagination. Memory is not a thing that happens to you; you create your memories. You can make any information into something more meaningful. When we start using the memory systems you will see how easy it is to convert abstract information into meaningful concepts. Using all these memory methods improves your creativity, enhances your memory and your humor too.

CHAPTER 6

USE YOUR CAR TO REMEMBER

*"Making the simple complicated is
commonplace; making the complicated
simple, awesomely simple, that's creativity."*

~ Charles Mingus

We have just learned to bring information to life by turning information into pictures or mind movies. Now we need to learn to create files, for pictures, from our long-term memory. This will assist us in remembering new information. These systems require you to think differently. I always think it is amazing how people want to improve their memory and concentration, but they do more of the same thing and expect a different result. You have to *do* different, to *become* different.

The method that I will share with you now is called, *The Car Method*. Our car is a great long-term storage compartment because we know it well and can easily navigate it in our mind. With this method, as with all of them, I want you to SEE the images in your mind. Remember every word in any language is only a picture drawn with letters. Get rid of your excuses like, "I'm not creative" or "I don't think like this". This isn't how I think either; this is how I have trained myself to think, because it works.

These methods may seem silly but just go with it. I promise that you will see the point and you will remember the information. These systems take long for me to explain, but they work at the speed of thought. The only reason it won't work for you, is if you don't do it.

We are going to use nouns for this exercise because they are easy to imagine and therefore easier to control and store. Then in the second exercise, and the rest of the book, we will use more abstract information. Follow the images in your mind and let's see how much you remember.

See your car in your mind and imagine you squeeze a big **apple** into the front grid of your car. Take a **carrot** and stab it into the bonnet. On the windscreen see **grainy bread**, and think to yourself, "The grainy bread is going to damage my windscreen wipers." Get inside your car and squash **dried fruit** on the dash board, really see it go into your speedometer. On the driver's seat imagine you are sitting on **blue berries** and **strawberries** – really feel it. Throw **eggs** at the person sitting in the passenger seat next to you, they now have egg on their face. Imagine you are pouring thousands of **nuts** and **seeds** onto your back seat. Go outside your car and imagine a massive **orange** on your roof. You open the boot and it is full of **fish** – really smell the fish. In the exhaust pipe there is **broccoli** and **Brussels sprouts** growing out of the exhaust, and finally the tires of your car are made out of **sweet potatoes**. Sweet!

Go through your car, from the beginning to the end, and see if you can remember all the information. If a word didn't stick, go back, make the connection stronger and SEE it more clearly in your mind.

What you have just learned are fourteen super foods; foods that have been shown to improve your vitality and keep your mind agile and alert. Not only do you know the list forwards but you also know it backwards and inside and out. What is on the roof? What are the car tires made of? What was on the driver's seat? What was on the bonnet of the car? Your mind automatically makes the connection and answers the question for recall. Now that you really know it, it is easier to use and think about.

Some people say, "But now I have to remember the car too, you are giving me more to remember." That is not true. With all of the systems you will be using something that is already in your memory. In fact, you are using all of the unused space in your long-term memory.

You remembered the entire list and with ease. Now, why does this system work so well? If you throw water into a sieve it goes in and straight through. If you put a packet into the sieve the water will get trapped. Your memory works in the same way. Your long-term memory (things that are in your memory forever, like your name and what your house looks like etc.) is like the packet that can be used to trap short-term information (new information coming in, like a new telephone number.) When you have managed to do that, you make a strong medium-term memory (MTM).

With the car list your whole car is in your long-term memory (LTM). LTM offers you a place to store the information. The locations in the car become storage compartments for the short-term memories (STM). All the memory methods work with my formula:

LTM + STM = MTM.

These methods also organize information, therefore making it easier to find. What is easier to remember, 'Super memory' or 'Yomerm puers'? Same letters, but very different meaning and the second is harder to memorize. The more order you put into a subject the easier it will be to remember.

The secret to accelerated learning is superior organization.

We can use other cars to remember other new information too. Here is a picture of a car with seven images on it. It shouldn't conflict with the food car, because it opens up a new 'memory file'.

Look at the picture below and make sure that you can clearly recreate the whole image in your mind. Break the images down; look at each place and make sure that each one sticks to its place.

Have you done that? Good, what you have just learned are Stephen Covey's *Seven Habits of Highly Effective People*. By remembering all seven images you are creating points of reference within your mind for each of the habits. When you have it in your memory it will be easier to gauge if you are living the Seven Habits. When you mentally look at the car you will instantly be able to recall all the information. Remember the more you know, the easier it is to get to know more.

Let me explain each of the pictures; the Seven Habits are as follows:

Habit 1: **Be Pro-active** – I thought of a Bee that is a pro-golfer. That picture should be enough to trigger habit 1.

Habit 2: **Begin with the End in Mind** – The brain is running a race, and looking at the end in mind.

Habit 3: **Put First Things First** – the man is in 1st position, putting first things first.

Habit 4: **Think Win/Win** – the two trophies show that everyone wins with win/win.

Habit 5: **Seek First to Understand, Then to be Understood** – The man *under* the umbrella will *stand* up.

Habit 6: **Synergize** – *sign* balancing on the *edge* with *eyes*.

Habit 7: **Sharpen the Saw** – on the tire of the car.

With your memory always use as few pictures as possible, to remember as much as possible. The more simple and clear it is, the less you will feel overwhelmed.

You can also make the connection that the first 3 habits are the **Private Victory**: the front of your car is private; you are the only one that opens the bonnet of your car. Habits 4, 5 and 6 are the **Public Victory**: in the car, you allow others to get into your car, it is public. Habit 7 is outside the car: the seventh habit keeps everything else in check.

Remember these habits, read the book to get more understanding and retention and live them. As Stephen Covey said, *"Habits can be learned and unlearned. But I also know it isn't a quick fix. It involves a process and a tremendous commitment."*

In this chapter you have been able to remember twenty-one bits of useful information. These methods help you to organize information more clearly and therefore you will be using more of your memory power and potential. All the methods in this book help you to store information that can be used. You can make many more storage compartments in and on your car. If you think about it you can use every detail of your car to find at least 100 places to store new information in your memory. You can also use any other forms of transport: buses, trains, airplanes, ships or even space ships as storage files or compartments.

CHAPTER 7

USE YOUR BODY TO REMEMBER

"The music of your life is far better played
with all the fingers of your Multiple
Intelligences performing their magic on the
keyboard of your existence."

~ Tony Buzan

The quote you have just read was taken from Tony's book called *Head First*. In his book he talks about how we have at least ten intelligences. We don't just have one way of being 'clever' but at least ten and probably more. I like to remember these intelligences to remind myself how incredible we all are and to focus on improving them daily. But before I get ahead of myself, let me demonstrate how to remember these intelligences with another system. It is called, *The Body Method*. It is similar to *The Car Method*, but this time we are using parts of our body to store the new information. Your body is another great long-term storage compartment; you are in it every day and you know it well. There are plenty of storage compartments that you can use, but for demonstration purposes I'm only going to use ten places.

With this method we are going to place ten key bits of information on our body. The information is a bit more abstract, it will require you to think more creatively, so let's give it a go.

The first place that we are going to store information on is our feet. The first intelligence is **Creative** intelligence. So I want you to imagine that you are standing on a big bright **light bulb** (a light bulb always reminds me of creative ideas), and it is burning your feet. To strengthen the association you can also imagine you are painting a beautiful work of art on your feet.

On the second place, your knees, we are going to store **Personal** intelligence. Now imagine a big **Purse** (sounds like Personal) on your knees. Create a bit of action with this picture; imagine opening the purse on your knees and your knees come flying out of it. Personal intelligence is about taking responsibility, so own the purse on your knees.

The next storage compartment is your thighs. Here we will store **Social** intelligence. Imagine people having a big **Party** (Social) on your thighs. Really SEE the party and feel it happening on your thighs now.

The next place is your belt or hips, and we will store **Spiritual** intelligence there. Imagine a beautiful **angel** on your belt, or that the angel is buckling your belt for you (Angels remind me of spirituality). Now review all the previous images from your feet to your hips. The words are Creative, Personal, Social, and Spiritual.

Next is your **Physical** intelligence and we will store it on your stomach. Imagine you get **physical**, start doing sit ups and your stomach all of a sudden becomes muscular; it becomes the perfect six pack.

Imagine in your left hand your **Sensual** intelligence. Here you can imagine a snotty nose, ears, and eyes to remind you of all of your **senses.**

Then in your right hand place **Sexual** intelligence – here you can make up your own picture.

Now let's review quickly, we have: Creative, Personal, Social, Spiritual, Physical, Sensual, and Sexual.

The next place is your mouth. Imagine big bright colorful numbers flying out of your mouth (**Numerical** intelligence). Or, you can only speak in **numbers.**

On your nose, SEE a space ship landing on your nose and forehead (**Spatial** intelligence.) Or, SEE a **space ship** flying up your nose.

Finally, on the top of your head imagine writing words on your hair, or your hair starts talking (**Verbal** intelligence.)

Let's review The Body List:

The Creative and Emotional Intelligences

(Legs create motion; that is to remind you that the Creative and Emotional intelligences are stored on your feet and legs.)

1. Creative intelligence
2. Personal intelligence (self-knowledge, self-fulfillment, and understanding self)
3. Social intelligence
4. Spiritual intelligence

The Bodily Intelligences

(All stored on the biggest part of your body, on your torso.)

5. Physical intelligence
6. Sensual intelligence
7. Sexual intelligence

The Traditional IQ Intelligences

(The head intelligences.)

8. Numerical intelligence
9. Spatial intelligence
10. Verbal intelligence

Tony Buzan says we are now entering the intelligence age, so it is vitally important that you know more about your amazing intelligences. The Body Method also helps you structure the information so that you can easily jump in and out of the material. When you read *Head First*, the body list will act as a powerful memory matrix that will attract more information and improve your understanding and recognition of the content. If you hear any other list of intelligences, like Howard Gardner's, you can easily slot the information into its relevant compartment. When you hear people discussing IQ you will also immediately know (remember) that IQ only tests three intelligences – the head intelligences.

> *"Most of us have been taught to think that we are either intelligent or we are not. But the definitions of intelligence we learned at school were built around the specific types of intelligence that are most valued at school – verbal intelligence and numerical intelligence."*
>
> *~ Paul McKenna*

The Body Method was originally invented by the ancient Greeks. You can use this method to remember information for exams, work, shopping lists or any list of information. You can even use it to remember things when you don't have a pen at hand, like when you are in the shower. I just used ten places as an example, but you can use your back, your ears, eyes, nose... you can use it all. Just make sure you connect the two in a humorous way (remember the SEE principles), and that you remember the order. I have been able to use this method to remember fifty bits of information. I like to use this system to remember information so that I can consistently look at the information and have it at my fingertips.

CHAPTER 8

PEGGING INFORMATION DOWN

*"The existence of forgetting has never been
proved: We only know that some things
don't come to mind when we want them."*

~ Friedrich Nietzsche

Have you ever had this experience, you smell
something and instantly your memory takes you
back to another time? The smell is a link to the
experience. Or, you hear a song and a whole stream of
memories are released from your mind?

We can consciously take control of this reminder
principle to create another system for our memory
skills toolbox. This is the first system that I ever
learned, and it introduced me to my memory potential.
It worked so well that it seemed like a trick and ever
since that day I have been hooked on the power of my

memory. I hope it has a similar effect for you. It is called, *The Peg Method* of memory.

We are going to explore the power of your associative mind. We are going to learn two new peg methods of memory. The first is called *The Rhyming Peg Method* and the other *The Shape Peg Method*. These secrets were brought to our conscious awareness by John Sambrook and Henry Heardson in the late 1700s.

These methods are very simple and effective. It will provide you with a method that can help you remember 40 or more bits of information in a short space of time. You can even remember the information in random order and by number.

Let me explain the first method, *the rhyming pegs*. The pegs act in much the same way as clothes pegs. They keep information hanging around in your mind. The pegs themselves must become part of your long-term memory for them to work. Remember you always need your long-term memory to assist your short-term memory. With this method you associate new information to long-term memory pegs in your mind. The pegs also act as compartments or files for your new thoughts. The method is simple; it makes memory pegs out of rhyming words and we will use the following rhyming words as mental files:

One rhymes with the word Bun

Two– Shoe

Three– Tree

Four– Door

Five– Hive

Six– Sticks

Seven– Heaven

Eight– Gate

Nine– Vine

Ten– Hen

Now, each one of these pegs can become compartments to store new information. You link the peg (using the SEE principle) to the words that you want to remember.

In Tony Robbins' life changing book, *Awaken the Giant Within*, he has a list of The Ten Emotions of Power. I want you to use this new system so that you can hold these emotions in your mind. Think about them daily, because personal development only happens when you can remember what you need to act on.

The Ten Emotions of Power are:

1. Love and warmth
2. Appreciation and gratitude
3. Curiosity
4. Excitement and passion
5. Determination
6. Flexibility
7. Confidence

8. Cheerfulness
9. Vitality
10. Contribution

Remember to make the images illogical. SEE the information in your mind for a few seconds. Take your time and make the associations strong; you can also draw an image to help you experience the information more.

One bun, imagine a heart (symbol for love) shaped warm bun, or imagine that thousands of warm hearts are flying out of a bun. Really visualize it and you will remember that one is **love and warmth**.

Two shoe, imagine that a preacher is grating a shoe with a cheese grater. I used a preacher to remind you of **appreciation** and a grater for **gratitude**.

Three tree, imagine a cat in the tree, don't make it logical. Maybe, imagine that the branches look like cats, cats are hanging off the branches or cats are growing out of the tree. Curiosity killed the cat. So, three is **curiosity**.

Four door, imagine an excited person bashing down your door. Or, the door is so excited it jumps up and down and opens and closes. Then you squeeze passion fruit on the excited door. Four is **excitement and passion**.

Five hive, imagine determined bees or determined terminators trying to break open a bee hive. Bees are a determined nation. **Determination** is five.

Six sticks, imagine hitting a flexible person, that is doing the splits, with a stick. Or, really feel how flexible the stick can be. Six is **Flexibility**.

Seven heaven, imagine heaven is full of confident people. See them walking tall with confidence that they are in paradise. Seven is **Confidence**.

Eight gate, see a smiley faced shaped gate. You cheerfully open the cheerful gate. Eight is **cheerfulness**.

Nine vine, see vitamins growing on a vine. As you eat these vitamin grapes you feel your sense of **vitality** improve.

Ten hen, imagine a hen giving you presents. She is a contributing hen. Ten is **contribution**.

Now really see each link picture in your mind and make it clear. You should now know these emotions forwards, backwards, and in random order. Test yourself to see if you have them all.

Practise feeling these emotions because you become good at what you practise. Tony Robbins says, *"You are the source of all your emotions; you are the one who creates them. Plant these emotions daily, and watch your whole life grow with vitality that you've never dreamed of before."*

71

The rhyme method can be extended by finding more words that rhyme with the number, e.g.: one - bun, sun, tum, gum and gun. With this method you can easily create a peg system that you can use to store up to 30 bits of new information.

Pegging also has no limits; you can create other lists too. Here is the second short peg list that you can use, *The Shape System*. It converts numbers into concrete shapes. It works in the same way as the rhyme list, only this time the pegs are shaped like the number. We are not going to do an exercise with this system, because you have already learned the principle in the rhyme list.

Use this list on your own, to remember ten bits of new information, play with it and have a bit of fun. The shape method just gives you another option to use. Here is the list:

These peg lists create so many new possibilities; you can create all kinds of peg lists. You can use any list that is already in your long-term memory.

You can make up words for each letter of the alphabet e.g. apple, bucket, cat, dolphin etc. Use any list that you already know well: your favorite football players, super heroes, pop stars or any list that you can remember in order. Enjoy using this method, and find new ways to improve it.

CHAPTER 9

IN THE FIRST PLACE

"Whatever you think about, that's what you remember. Memory is the residue of thought."

~ Daniel T. Willingham

The system that you are about to discover is the most incredible tool you will ever learn. It will help you grow in ways that you could never imagine. It is so simple, it has been around for 2500 years, and yet few have harnessed its potential. You can use this system to remember any information and mountains of it. It takes practice, but once you use it you will never look back.

This method is the original and still the most effective of all the systems. Using this system is as easy as remembering a journey. Some people think this method is too simple to work, but it works because it doesn't overwhelm you.

It is the same process as *The Car* and *Body* List, but only this time we are using places or markers on a location, journey or route to store information.

Here is how it works:

1) Prepare in your mind an organized location (e.g. a house layout, a journey or a shopping centre.)

2) Create markers or places on this location, same as what we did with the body and car list (in an easy-to-follow order.)

3) Make a clear image (using the SEE principles) of the information that you would like to remember.

4) Place each item you are trying to remember on each of the marked locations.

In short, it is as simple as finding a place like a route, journey or building in your mind to store the information. Then you store it. This system makes remembering large amounts of information as easy as remembering a trip to the nearest shop. You are using the formula again: **Long-Term Memory + Short-Term Memory = Medium-Term Memory**.

Let me introduce you to *The Journey Method* with a short exercise. We are going to store twelve useful principles from one of John C. Maxwell's books. I really enjoy his books because they are always very well organized and therefore making storing information easier. He normally creates a summary list of the topics that he will cover and then he writes in more detail about each topic. You can use the systems to remember all of his lists and laws and become an expert in leadership. Once the information is in a memorable matrix, it will start to attract more information to it; it helps long-term storage and use. When you have it in your head it is so much easier to use, because what is the use of learning information if you can't recall what you know?

In his book *Today Matters* he shares twelve keys that you can focus on daily to get more success and fulfillment in your life. As he says, *"You will never change your life until you change something you do daily."* He calls them, The Daily Dozen.

Here are the keys:

1. Attitude
2. Priorities
3. Health
4. Family
5. Thinking
6. Commitment
7. Finances
8. Faith
9. Relationships
10. Generosity
11. Values
12. Growth

Most people will repeat the list of information over and over again and try to force it into their memory. Rote learning and constant repetition creates an aversion to learning and it is frustrating. The more you can encode information into your memory, the more effective the learning. Let's use a method to find the fun in **FrUstratioN**. Now all that we have to do is to focus attention and connect each thought to a place. Try this little exercise with me...

I am going to be using four rooms in my house as a journey to give you an example of how you can use this system. The rooms are compartments in my mind that I can use to store new information. Let me guide you through the house and let's store the information together.

Make sure that your markers are all in an easy to follow order. Then review your markers to make sure you have clear storage compartments. The places must also be near each other, but nicely spaced out.

Here is a mental map of four rooms in my house and twelve places that we will use, and they are:

Room 1 Kitchen: 1. Washing machine 2. Fridge 3. Stove.

Room 2 TV room: 4. Chairs 5. TV 6. Exercise bike.

Room 3 Bedroom: 7. Mirror 8. Cupboards 9. Bed.

Room 4 Bathroom: 10. Bath 11. Shower 12. Toilet.

Room 1 (Kitchen)	Room 2 (TV room)
Washing Machine Fridge Stove	Chairs Exercise bike TV

Room 3 (Bedroom)	Room 4 (Bathroom)
Mirror Bed Cupboards	Bath Toilet Shower

If I gave you a box with twelve objects in it, would you be able to place it on the furniture in my house? Of course you would, now all we do is turn the information into something tangible, like an object, and then place them in the room.

We start in the kitchen. The first word is **Attitude**. Imagine someone with a really bad attitude jumping into your washing machine. Clean up his attitude in the machine. SEE it!

At the next place imagine writing all of your **Priorities** on the fridge door. Use a permanent marker and think about how your priorities are permanently stored on the fridge door.

Imagine a healthy bodybuilder making an apple pie and shoving it into the stove. The apples are also a reminder for **Health**.

So what was in the washing machine? On the fridge? At the stove?

Now we move to the TV room. The first place there is the chairs. Imagine your whole **Family** is jumping up and down on the chairs. The more illogical the image, the more it will stick.

The second place is the TV. Imagine a thought bubble coming out of the TV, because it is a **Thinking** machine. It also influences our thinking.

The final place in the room is the exercise bike, so imagine combing (reminds you of commitment) the exercise bike. It is also a **Commitment** to use the bike.

In my bedroom the first place is the mirror and here imagine money flying out of the mirror. Your **Finances** are a mirror of your productivity.

Whatever represents faith for you, place it inside the cupboard. Put **Faith** on every shelf or hanger.

The next word we want to place on our memory journey is **Relationships**, and that is on the bed. Okay, you can make your own picture here.

The final room is the bathroom. See a genie jumping out of the bath and he gives you what you wish. The genie giving reminds us of **Generosity**.

Imagine the shower is made out of gold. Or, you open the taps and gold runs out of it. Gold has great value, and represents **Values**.

At the last place we imagine a tree growing out of the toilet for **Growth**.

What was the word connected to each place?

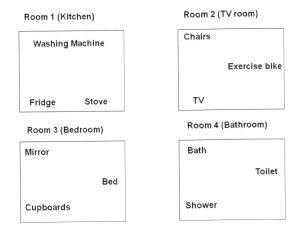

Excellent, that is now your first memory route or journey, and it will begin to open your mind to the possibility of having a perfect memory. You have just learnt the 12 keys in John Maxwell's book *Today Matters*, and it was as easy as walking around my house. You will remember all the words if you have connected them properly. Go through it a few times and you will know The Daily Dozen. You will get better results with this method if you used your own environment because you are more aware of the order of the places.

Review the list backwards and you will notice that it will all still be there. By reviewing it backwards, you make the images clearer for your memory. If you made clear images and placed them on the route, the list will be very memorable. This method helps you to see the big picture and zoom into the details. The concepts are brought to life and become concrete. It is always easier to remember something that is experienced in your mind; we remember what we think about.

Now think about this information that you have learned, buy *Today Matters* and focus on making small changes in these areas daily, and remember it to live it.

This journey or route method shows you what is possible. Every great memory person uses this method more than any other. It is so effective because you can make thousands of storage places. Think about how many markers you can make? We all have a brilliant memory for journeys. You have visited many places in your life; you can use buildings, museums, schools, shopping centers, and almost any location that you know. Make sure they are places you know well, that have significance to you, and they have lots of variety. You can make your routes as long as you want; you can have a place or route for every subject you are learning. Remember to have fun!

This system will change the way that you learn forever. The only effort is trying to improve your ability to make images and placing it on a familiar mental journey. It will feel like you are cheating; it is like having crib notes or a teleprompter inside your head. The journey is like the paper and the images are like the ink. Your imagination can create any information on a familiar journey. It will change your life!

You can use it to remember all kinds of information, I have helped medical students, law students, pilots, managers, and business people remember all kinds of information with this method. I used this method to store the first 10,000 digits of pi. A friend of mine Dr. Yip Swee Chooi remembered the entire Oxford dictionary, 1774 pages, word-for-word with this method. Anyone can store an unlimited amount if they choose to spend the time. Some people say, "I will run out of space." If I gave you a truck full of objects to place in a shopping mall, would you be able to do that? Of course you would. If you look for it, you will find thousands and thousands of places just waiting to be used in your mind. There are no limits to this system, only limits in your own thinking.

The important thing is that you practise. The more you practise the better you will get.

CHAPTER 10

LINKING THOUGHTS

*"No memory is ever alone; it's at the end of
a trail of memories, a dozen trails that each
have their own associations."*

~ Louis L'Amour

In the previous chapters we learned to bring information to life, and to store it in a long-term memory compartment system. Now in this chapter we are going to learn to link more thoughts together. It is a way to direct attention and to strengthen your imagination and your ability to associate concepts. Your mind is an associating machine and it has no limits.

I often hear people say, "Oh, do you learn by association?" The answer to that is we only learn by association. Learning is connecting new information to old information, it doesn't happen any other way. It is creating a relationship between the known and the unknown – and the more you know, the easier it is to connect more information and get to know more.

Now let's memorize a list together to experience this method. It will seem silly, but stick with it and I will make a point. This story takes longer for me to explain than what happens in your mind. Read it and remember to use the SEE principle.

I want you to imagine that you are **washing a tin**; really see it in your mind. As you wash the tin, it suddenly begins developing a huge **Adams** apple. A **chef** and **her son** grab the Adams apple and rip it out. The Chef and her son then decide to make some **medicine**, which they give to Marilyn **Monroe** and she starts to develop a massive **Adams** apple too. Michael **Jackson** sees her Adams apple throbbing and runs away screaming and jumps into a **van** with **beer in** it. The van is being driven by a big yellow **hairy sun** – really see it, make it silly, hairy, and let it stick. The hairy sun doesn't drive very well and crashes into a **tiler** tilling his wall. The tiler's tiles are **polka** dot tiles. A **tailor** takes the polka dots off and starts tailoring you a polka-dotted suite.

Now recall the story and all the key words. If you didn't get it all, read it again and make the links stronger. See if you can do it backwards too.

What you have just learned are the first twelve presidents of the USA. You can continue remembering all 44 Presidents just by linking one thought to the next. If you have any problems recalling the list just make it more outstanding and make the links clearer.

Here is the list of the first twelve Presidents:

1. **Washing** a **tin** - Washington
2. **Adams** apple - **Adams**
3. A **chef** and **her son** - sounds like **Jefferson**
4. **Medicine** - sounds like **Madison**
5. Marilyn **Monroe** - **Monroe**
6. **Adams** apple - **Adams**
7. Michael **Jackson** - **Jackson**
8. A **van** with **beer in** - **Van Buren**
9. A **hairy sun** - **Harrison**
10. A **tiler** (a person who lays tiles) - **Tyler**
11. **Polk**a dots - **Polk**
12. **Tailor** - **Taylor**

Once you have the list in your mind go through it forwards and backwards a few times to make sure it is all there. You can also link more information to the list, so it becomes like a new peg list. You could link each vice-president to your presidents, just like we did with the foreign words and capitals. You can also connect your links or stories to some of the other systems that you have learnt. You can link more than one concept at a specific place or compartment on the car, body, pegs or journey method. This way you can remember thousands of words or concepts by connecting links to a short mental journey.

It is so powerful because we use more of our creativity and imagination to make the information outstanding, therefore stimulating our interest and curiosity; keeping our attention at a peak. Each word reminds you of the next, you are making your **own links** and you are only memorizing two things at a time. You can also use this method to memorize paragraphs of information. All that you have to do is condense everything down to a list of key words and then convert those lists into meaningful link stories. A whole syllabus or a book can be condensed into a ridiculous story. When you do this it is easy to remember, giving you a great mental workout and it is fun!

CHAPTER 11

REMEMBERING NAMES

"Remember that a person's name is to that person the sweetest and most important sound in any language."

~ Dale Carnegie

There is no such thing as a good or bad memory for names, there is only a good or a bad strategy. In this chapter you are going to learn strategies that can make a huge difference to your name memory. Make a commitment today to improve; it is a commitment that will provide you with numerous benefits and save you from many embarrassing situations.

In Chapter 3, I showed you the self-fulfilling circle. Get rid of your limiting beliefs about your name memory and start to focus on finding a strategy that can help you. Become motivated and interested in names and how we brand people according to that name.

Imagine you meet a person and they say that they will give you a million dollars if you could remember their name a week from today. Would you then remember it? Of course you would. We are all brilliant at names if we are motivated enough to hold on to them.

The methods that I will be sharing with you have been used for centuries. They require you to think differently and to use your incredible associating mind. Some people say that they have tried association to remember names and it doesn't work for them. It doesn't work if you don't practise, nothing in life works unless you work with it.

All the memory champions are using association methods and can easily remember about a hundred names in less than half-an-hour. I believe that if you copy the strategies of the champions you can get the same results and if you don't you won't.

The untrained memory is not very reliable. The average person leaves their memory to chance, hoping that the name will somehow stick. The strategies that I will share with you work – use them!

Now if you want to remember names like a memory master you have to focus on the four Cs.

1. CONCENTRATE

When you meet someone with the same name as you, do you remember their name? Yes, because you are interested in that name, you always hear it, and your attention is at a peak. The name has meaning to you and you also connect it to yourself. If you follow this basic strategy with every person that you meet you will remember their names.

When we get introduced to people they normally say their name so quickly that nobody can get it. Take control of the introduction, to be able to really get the name you have to slow down the introduction. Put your elephant ears on and really hear the name, make remembering names something that is important to you.

Oliver Wendel Holmes said, *"A person must get a thing before they can forget it."* You need to really hear the name first, if you don't hear something you will not remember it. You have to first get it to turn it into a memory. If you hear the name, and repeat it back to the person you will improve your recall. If you don't hear the name, ask the person to say it to you again, and if it is a difficult name ask the person to spell the name too.

Listen and get genuinely interested in the other person's name. We are normally so worried about being interesting, that we forget to be interested. When you become interested you will want to listen to the name. Learn to listen to people from their perspective and not your own. Not only will it improve your name memory, but your social intelligence too.

2. CREATE

You have to create an image for the name in your mind, to be able to re-create it later.

Have you ever heard people say, "I know the face, but I can't remember the name...?" You never hear people say, "The face is on the tip of my tongue". We remember faces because they form an image in our mind. The names don't normally 'stick' because we try to remember it with our auditory memory or our little voice. It doesn't make sense to try to stick a sound to a vision – of course it won't stick. Plus, auditory memories are never as solid as visual memories.

To hold on to a memory we must make an image out of the name. Remember how we created images out of names when we learned the presidents? When you give a name meaning you can then hold on to it.

When you put a name into your mind and you don't do anything with it, it will disappear and you won't be able to find it again. This is because working memory doesn't store information. So to store it you need assistance from your short and long-term memory. You have to really think about the name to remember it because **we only remember what we think about.**

When you are introduced to someone, you only have twenty seconds to think about the name and make an association. If you don't do anything with the name in twenty seconds the name will be gone. The more connections and meaning you can give the name, the more it will 'stick'.

Some of the names will naturally create a picture like the surnames Baker, Cruise or Gardner. My surname is Horsley so you can think of a **horse** and Bruce **lee**. My first name is Kevin and it sounds like Cave in, making it easy to create an image and meaning out of my name. Other names may be more difficult, but by using a bit of creativity any name can be given meaning and turned into a picture.

3. CONNECT

Remember that all learning is creating a relationship between the known and the unknown. You will already know the face so you need to connect the unknown name to the known face. When you see the face it must act as a trigger or peg to bring the name to your awareness.

Here are some methods to make the connection. All the methods you learn here take a great deal longer to explain than to use.

COMPARISON CONNECTION

With this method you connect the person to a name that you already know. Let's say we meet a person by the name of George. To make the name stick, we think of someone that we already know with the same name. Do you know another George? You may even think of someone famous with the same name, like George Clooney.

Now all we do in our mind is compare the two people. What color hair does the George that we are meeting have? What color is the other George's hair? By comparing this one feature you will be paying more attention than you would have before, therefore making a stronger connection.

Compare as many different features as you can and you will focus your attention and create a long-term impression for perfect recall. It is as simple as that... just compare the two faces in your mind and you will remember them. Impact your memory even more by imagining the person with two heads – their own, and that of the person you already know with the same name.

I like this method because it helps you to both remember the new person, as well as reinforce the other name too. This method only takes a few seconds to help you remember the person's name forever. We are using the memory principle of taking a long-term name and using it to remember the short-term new name.

Some people ask, what happens if you don't have a similar name to compare to? We can then use one of the other methods that I will be showing you now. Find a system that works best for you.

FACE CONNECTION

With this method you make a link between the name and an outstanding feature on the person's face. Every person's face is unique and every face has an outstanding feature. Let me give you an example, imagine you are introduced to a woman and the first thing you notice about her face is that she has striking blue eyes. That will then be her outstanding feature. When she gives you her name you will then have a place to put the name. Imagine she says her name is Janice. You then make an image of the name: Janice sounds like **chain ice**. You then make the connection and think of a **chain** of **ice** flying out of her blue eyes.

Here is another example, imagine you meet a man and you notice that he has a big nose and his name is Peter. Turn the name into a picture; you can then imagine a 'Pea eater'. Then quickly make the connection that his nose is a big pea eater. By making a silly memorable association you will connect the face and the name together.

With this method never tell anybody what you have done in your mind. It is personal and some people may become offended. I remember once meeting a woman by the name of Hazel. She asked me how I remembered her name, so I told her... big mistake. I said I thought of a hazelnut. She was not impressed. Remember, most people identify with their names – they like it and consider it as their own unique brand. If you make fun of it you are making fun of them.

A few questions that people ask about this system are:

What happens if I meet four people and all of them have an outstanding nose?

Searching for the outstanding feature helps you focus on the face as you may never have done before. Most people never really look at the person when they are meeting them. So the feature is more about directing your focus on the face and making a connection. I have done a demonstration where I have remembered over a hundred names in half-an-hour using this method. When you meet a hundred people you use many of the same features, but amazingly there is never any confusion.

Go to Facebook to practise this method, there are millions of faces to choose from.

Can I connect the name to the clothes of a person?

Yes, but only if you notice the person's face too. People change clothes, but their faces are unique and don't change much.

What happens if I find it hard to make a mental picture of the person's name?

You can imagine writing their name on their forehead. Make sure you use a big fat red mental pen. It is all about creativity.

If you **create their name in your mind**, you will remember the name with as much ease as you remember the face.

MEETING LOCATION CONNECTION

When we meet people for the first time we tend to also remember the place that we first met them. The place makes a clear impression in our memory, but the name is nowhere to be found!

With this method we connect the name to the place where we meet the person. We are using a journey peg to hold on to the name. Let's say we meet a woman by the name of Rose. Ask yourself, "What will I remember about this place where I meet her?" Let's say you think you will remember the buffet table, you then connect a big red rose to it and when you think of the place you will think of her name.

4. CONTINUOUS USE

If you concentrate and get the name, then make it meaningful and connect it to the person, then this will enable you to remember the name for the short-term. However, to make the name stick in your memory forever you have to continue using it.

Talk about the name. If it is a foreign name ask the person what it means. How do you spell it?

Also, use the name in conversation. The more you talk about the name the less you will be relying on working memory and you will begin to store it.

In your mind ask yourself, "What is that person's name again?" Get the answer and then ask yourself, "Does that feel right?" Try to strengthen the association during the course of the day or evening.

Review the name. Create a names folder in your diary, on your computer or on your mobile phone of people that you would like to remember. Invite people you want to remember to one of your social networking sites, so that you can review their names. Review the names often to keep them in your long-term memory. It is just a question of writing the name down and where you met the person. Look at the list every now and again and you will have a massive name memory filing system, you will never be caught off guard for a name again.

You can use these methods to remember hundreds of people at one meeting. They are all designed to improve your focus of attention, because when you remember others they make a point of remembering you.

CHAPTER 12

REMEMBERING NUMBERS

*"Group a list of letters together and you
have a word that represents something – an
image, an emotion, a person. Throw a few
numbers together and you have, well, you
have another number."*

~ Dominic O'Brien

Numbers have become an important part of our lives, yet no one has shown us how to remember them.

You can use external memory devices to remember numbers and you can choose to outsource your brain. But if you are in business and you can recall facts and figures without referring to your 'external brain' or notes, then it builds trust and certainty.

When you remember facts and figures it builds confidence in your memory, it builds mental strength, and it is like gym for your brain.

If you call out digits, the average person will only remember about seven digits forwards and only four to five backwards.

If you have a trained memory there are no limits. I can remember a 50-digit random number in less than 20 seconds and 100 digits in 45 seconds. I have taken my number memory far beyond all the limits that have been set in that area.

Any person can produce the same results if they know the strategy. If you practise the methods and take pride in improving your memory, you can also develop these 'super-human powers'.

Many people try to repeat numbers over and over again, trying to hold on to the number for dear life. They do more of what they have always done to try to improve their recall.

We don't only improve with practice; if you repeat a bad habit over and over it just gets worse. You also need a new method. We could use *The Number Shape* method to hold on to smaller numbers, but the method I am about to show you has so many more possibilities and applications.

What is easier to remember?

1. American Presidential Candidates

or

2. 34729401215721110

It is obviously "American Presidential Candidates", it is easily understood. As soon as you say it you memorize it. It has meaning and makes a visual image in your mind. The number has no meaning, and it is not very memorable. So to remember numbers you need to give them more meaning.

The systems that the memory masters use vary, but most of them use a system where you change the numbers into words and then into images.

We take the numbers and twist them into shapes, so that they form letters. Then we turn the letters into words. This system seems like a lot of work but once you have your code down it will make the process of remembering numbers a breeze. The code almost memorizes itself; stick with it and open your mind to a whole new language. It is also a great way to exercise your verbal and numerical intelligence at the same time.

Let's get started with learning the number code. Just go with this process, it will all come together in a moment. Let us begin with the vowels **a, e, i, o** and **u**. These letters have no value. They act as fillers or blanks. The letters **w, h** and **y** are also fillers or blanks. They also have no value. Just remember that for now.

Now, see the numbers in the following letters:

0 is the **S, Z or C** sound: S sounds like the hissing of a wheel (which looks like 0):

1 represents the **T or D** sound:

2 is the **N** sound:

3 is the **M** sound:

If I make the word **TOMATOES**, what will the number be?

T: 1, O: no value, **M: 3**, A: no value, **T: 1**, O: no value, E: no value and **S: 0**. The number would be **1310**.

What word could you make for **321**?

3: M, **2: N** and **1: D or T**. We have the letters MNT or MND. If we add the vowel 'i' we have the word **Mint**, or if we add a 'd' at the end and the vowel 'e' we have **Mend**. Or, try the vowel 'a' and add a 'y', then you can make the name **Mandy**.

It is like learning a new number language.

4 is the **R** sound:

5 is the **L** sound:

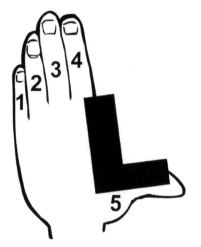

6 is the **J, Sh, soft Ch or soft G** sound:

What word can you make with **654**?

Jail**er**.

7 is the **K, C** sound:

8 is the **F or V** sound:

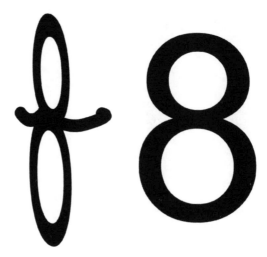

9 is the **B or P** sound, looks like the mirror and upside down image of 9:

If I say **cave**, what is the number?

78.

What word can you make with the number **98**?

Beef.

Now you can see that the number

3472 9401215 721110 is as easy as remembering

aMeRiCaN PReSiDeNTiaL CaNDiDaTeS

Do you now see how you can use this to remember any number?

You may be saying, "But now I have to remember a number and a word." No, it is like learning how to read. In the beginning you really have to work hard to encode the information, but then it becomes easy. Think of the number 007, instantly you think of James Bond. We are trying to create the same experience with all numbers that you want to remember. We remember concrete information with ease, so you are not remembering more; you are just making it more memorable.

It will take a bit of time to master, but once you have it you will have it forever.

I will now give you a list of words for each number from 1 to 100.

This method is great because you don't have to worry about spelling – it works on sounds.

00.**Sauce**

01. **So**d**a**

02. **Sun**

03. **Swim**

04. **Sir**

05. **Seal**

06. **Sash**

07. **Sock**

08. **Safe**

09. **Soap**

1. **Tie**

2. **Noah**

3. **Ma**

4. **Ray**

5. **Law**

6. **Jaw**

7. **Key**

8. **Foe, UFO**

9. **Bee**

10. **Toes**

11. **Dad**

12. **Tan**

13. **Dam**

14. **Deer**

15.Tail

16.Dish

17.Duck

18.Dove

19.Tape

20.Nose

21.Net

22.Nun

23.Gnome (Silent G)

24. Nero

25.Nail

26.Nosh

27.Neck

28.Navy

29. Nap

30. Mouse

31. Mat

32.Moon

33.Memo

34.Mower

35.Mail

36.Mash

37.Mike

38.Mafia

39.Map

40.Rose

41.Rat

42.Rain

43.Ram

44.Rower

45.Reel

46.Rash

47.Rock

48.Roof

49. Robe

50. Lassie(one S sound)

51. Lady

52.Lion

53.Limo

54.Lorry (one R sound)

55.Lily

56.Leach

57.Lock (ck one K sound)

58.Leaf

59.Lip

60.Chess (one S sound)

61.Jet

62.Chain

63.Jam

64.Chair

65.Jail

66.Cha – Cha

67.Shake

68.Chief

69. Jeep

70. Case

71. Cat

72.Can

73.Comb (Silent B)

74.Car

75.Coal

76.Cash

77.Coke

78.Cave

79.Cab

80.Face

81.**Fat**

82.**Fan**

83.**Foam**

84.**Fire**

85.**Foil**

86.**Fish**

87.**Fake**

88.Woof-woof

89. **FBI**

90. **Bus**

91. **Bat**

92.**Bun**

93.**Bum**

94.**Bear**

95.**Ball** (one L sound)

96.**Beach**

97.**Back**

98.**Beef**

99.**Baby**

100.**Daisies**

If you don't like some of the above words make up your own.

Not only can you use this method to remember numbers, but it can also be used as a very effective giant peg memory system.

This peg list memorizes itself. Memorize 10 a day. Let's say you want to memorize 10 to 15. For 10, the word is: toes. Think of the 1 as T and the 0 as S, then add vowels to make the word **T**oe**s**. Make a clear image of toes in your mind. For 11, think of the digits 1 1, that is: D and D. Now fit in a vowel and we have **Dad**. See it clearly in your mind. When we get to 15 we can make the word **doll** – remember the system works with the sounds of the word, so the LL sounds like one L. I prefer to use the word tail.

There are many advantages to knowing this method of memory. You can use it to learn 100 bits of information easily and in order. Once you have these values you can remember any numbers and there is no limit. When each number represents an image you can hold the number in your mind and place it on a system to remember as many numbers as you choose.

I have also used this method to remember athletic and sports statistics, stock prices, and any key information relating to numbers. This method also works well to remember important dates in history. I enjoy remembering dates because it links historical events to a time line. Once this information is in your memory it is easy to correlate it to other events. With this method, I am able to remember up to 100 dates in five minutes.

Plus, this is just another method that allows you to trap your thoughts and make information easier to recall.

Here is how dates are remembered:

1926 Television was first demonstrated.

The way I remember this one is to only remember the last three digits, because most of the dates we need to remember are all in the last thousand years. We take the 926 and use the code to make the word **Punch**. Now using the memory principles we can imagine that you punch the television and it starts to work.

1969 People land on the moon.

We can see a **Bishop** (969) on the moon. See a bishop walking on the moon and playing with the moon dust.

1901 The Nobel Prize was first awarded.

We can imagine that the first prize was made of **Pasta** (901).

1942 The first computer was developed.

We can imagine a computer that looks like a **Barn** (942).

1801 The first submarine was built.

See the submarine being built very **Fast** (801).

1784 The first newspaper was published.

See **Caviar** (784) all over the newspaper.

This number method was developed in the 1700s by a man named Stanislaus Mink von Wennshein who brought it to our conscious awareness. This method takes practice. You have to really work with it to make it work for you; then there will be no limits to your number memory and it will make you more knowledgeable.

CHAPTER 13

ART IN MEMORY

"Interest level is measured by how much you remember."

~ Philip A. Bossert

In this chapter, I want to show you the power of turning information into art. All of the systems taught in this book can be enhanced by turning them into a drawing, painting or picture. When you use more of your creativity you will be using more of your memory. It is a very simple method – you take information and you simply turn it into some form of art, and the information is remembered forever. It grabs your attention and your mind won't let go.

As I have said before, every word is a picture drawn with letters. Every word can conjure up an image that can be drawn, and pictures register very quickly in the brain. If an image can be presented in 3D it adds to the visual impact because that is the way things appear in the real world. You can achieve this by using Google images, by getting an illustrator to make you drawings, you can cut out pictures from magazines, or you can just use doodles. Any art can help you to remember more. You can sculpt your information; you can paint it, or even act it out. The whole process is about creative remembering and becoming more associated and personally involved with the information.

Use the power of Google images to create memory diagrams. Place all the images in a Word or PowerPoint document and view it often, so that when you look at the picture it creates instant learning. Let me give you two examples - the pictures on the next page are not professionally drawn it is just a whole bunch of Google images placed together to make a linked picture.

Have a look at the pictures and see how much registers in your mind. Link the pictures in a story and it will create an even stronger connection. The more deeply you think about any information, the more you will remember it.

This picture on the next page is a memory diagram of the twelve cranial nerves that emerge directly from our brain:

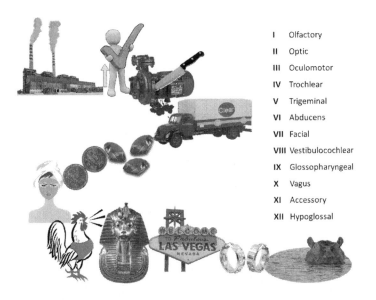

I	Olfactory
II	Optic
III	Oculomotor
IV	Trochlear
V	Trigeminal
VI	Abducens
VII	Facial
VIII	Vestibulocochlear
IX	Glossopharyngeal
X	Vagus
XI	Accessory
XII	Hypoglossal

The link starts with a picture of an **old factory** (sounds like **Olfactory**). The second picture is a man picking **up** a right **tick** to remind you of **Optic**. The third picture is a motor with a knife in it; it is **a killer motor** (sounds like **Oculomotor**). The fourth picture is a **truck**, with **clear** written on it, which represents **Trochlear**. The **three gems** are a reminder for **Trigeminal**. **Two cents** for **Abducens**. A lady having a **facial** is for **Facial**. **Vest** being worn by a **cock** for **Vestibulocochlear** – you can always add more to the picture if the picture doesn't trigger the whole word. The **pharaoh** has red lip **gloss** on for **Glossopharyngeal**. The Las **Vegas** sign, for the **Vagus** nerve. The earrings are an **Accessory** and finally the **hippo** with red lip **gloss** is for **Hypoglossal**.

These pictures are all short mental reminders or triggers to help you recall the main content. By looking, linking, and locking in the image you will make the memory link stronger and easier to recall. Try it!

The next example is a picture that will help you remember the first ten elements of the periodic table:

First, we have a shiny yellow fire hydrant (**Hydrogen**) with helium-filled balloons (**Helium**) tied to the top of the hydrant. The helium balloons are touching the light bulb (**Lithium**). The light bulb is burning the different colored berries (**Beryllium**). The berries are being eaten by a smelly wild boar (**Boron**). A car with a bun attached to it (**Carbon**), crashes into the boar. Behind the car-bun is a knight (**Nitrogen**), and out of his armor pops a scuba diving oxygen tank (**Oxygen**). The oxygen tank is being used by the woman with flu

(**Fluorine**). The spluttering and sneezing 'flu woman' has a massive neon sign (**Neon**) that blinks on and off behind her.

Look at the picture again, make the links and it will be installed in your memory.

If you wanted to remember the entire periodic table, you could create a few pictures and it will all be installed.

You can also use memory diagrams to help children remember spelling. Here are a few examples:

Business

There are two snakes (**2 S**s) in the de**ss**ert.

Here is a great way to clear up any confusion between homophones:

He has a **pear** in his **ear**.

The **pair** of shoes are flying through the **air**.

Any information can be represented as a drawing, painting, photograph or sculpture. Make an effort to turn key information that you need for your life into a picture so that you will be able to easily see it in your mind's eye. Use art to remember... and have fun!

Another great way to get your creative brain working for planning and remembering is:

Mind Mapping™ (Registered trademark by Tony Buzan)

> *"Your memory system operates so quickly*
> *and effortlessly that you seldom notice it*
> *working."*
>
> *~ Daniel T. Willingham*

One of the best ways to watch your mind and memory at work is through Mind Mapping. When you adopt this method into your life it will change the way you think. It is a powerful way to organize information, to think on paper, and get more out of your head.

Tony Buzan is the inventor of Mind Maps and has authored over 80 books. He created this amazing mind tool in the early 1970s and the method has evolved into one of the world's most effective learning and thinking tools.

Tony calls Mind Mapping the 'Swiss army knife for the brain.' It is not only a method for expanding your memory, but a way to improve your thinking skills. Mind Mapping can be used for: memorizing, learning, presenting, communicating, organizing, planning, meetings, negotiating, and all types of thinking.

A Mind Map is a multi-sensory way of transferring your thoughts to paper. It is incredibly easy and simple to use. At first it may take a bit of practice, but then your brain will remember how to have fun, and your life and learning will never be the same again. Mind Maps are a wonderful way of structuring information, so that you can see the big picture and the details. With linear notes, which are lists and lines, you will never have the flexibility that you have with Mind Maps.

To be a successful Mind Mapper all you need is the following:

1. Your brain;
2. A blank piece of paper, the bigger the better, and turn it to landscape;
3. Lots of colored pens and pencils.

The best way to explain a Mind Map is to map something out. The Mind Map that I will be creating here is about all the systems that I have shared with you in this book.

With every Mind Map you start in the centre of a blank page with a central image. This central image is what the whole Mind Map is about; therefore I will call this central image 'Systems'. As we now know images are memorable and stimulate more creativity.

Step 1:

Step 2:

Once you have your central image, then you connect branches to the central image and start branching out the headings. The main branches are all the memory systems we have covered.

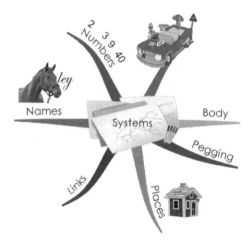

Step 3:

Once we have our main branches, then we can connect second and third level branches to give more detail to each main branch.

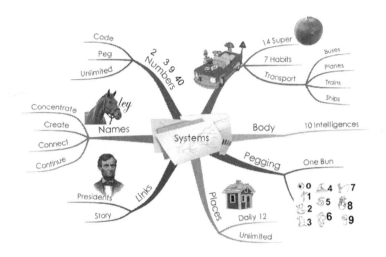

We can add even more branches to the existing branches to help clarify ideas or give more detail. Remember to use only one word per branch. This aids your associating mind to bloom freely, and remember to add lots of images. Each main branch will also have one color, this helps visually to distinguish between different branches or content. A Mind Map can never end because your associating mind can always find just one more memory.

Mind Maps are entertaining; they are fun and make use of your creative brain. If you choose to stick with it, you will take your mind to a new level. You will improve your creativity, planning power, develop more of your brain, and increase your powers of memory and observation. You can use Mind Maps for a whole range of learning areas; they can be used very effectively to summarize large amounts of information, and to get the gist of what is being communicated.

Here is a Mind Map that I made of the book *The Seven Habits of Highly Effective People*.

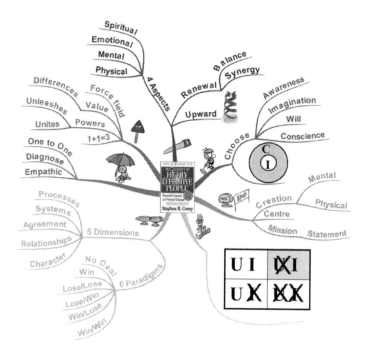

You will notice that each main branch shows a concept that we remembered on *The Car List*. This Mind Map summarizes the key content from Stephen Covey's whole book.

I created this Mind Map with iMindMap software. There are many Mind Mapping computer programs out there, but nothing comes close to the flexibility and usability of iMindMap. Play with it, you will be surprised at how much you can achieve with this one thinking tool.

CHAPTER 14

USING THE METHODS

"Success is neither magical nor mysterious.
Success is a natural consequence of
consistently applying basic fundamentals."

~ Jim Rohn

Now that you know the fundamentals of the memory methods you can succeed with any information. By being more creative with information it helps increase your involvement with the content, and makes it part of your reality, therefore improving your memory. In this chapter I want to share with you how you can adapt the methods to remember almost anything. I will give you short guidelines on how to remember information word-for-word, remember presentations, how to get rid of your absent mindedness, remember playing cards, and how to remember anything that you choose to study.

1. REMEMBERING WRITTEN INFORMATION WORD-FOR-WORD

> *"Memory ...is the diary that we all carry about with us."*
>
> *~ Oscar Wilde*

This is the method that I use to remember information word-for-word. If you work with this method you will be able to remember any written information with ease. You can use it to remember quotes, poems, definitions or verses from religious text.

Remembering information verbatim can help you in presenting, negotiations or meetings. You can also use it to hold on to information so that you can call upon it when you need a bit of inspiration. It is also helpful in exams to remember key definitions of key concepts.

Remembering and reciting poems is also a great way to train your mind and improve your presentation ability. Many religious texts refer to the importance of holding verses in your heart, so that you can live the lessons being taught.

In this section we will be using a quote called *Success* that has been attributed to Ralph Waldo Emerson. The first element of this memory method is to find the key words that will help you remember the rest of the text. Have a look at the key words that I have picked out:

SUCCESS

To **laugh often** and much; to win the respect of **intelligent people** and the **affection of children**; to earn the **appreciation of honest critics** and endure the **betrayal of false friends**; to appreciate **beauty**, to find the **best in others**; to **leave the world** a bit better, whether by a **healthy child**, a **garden patch** or a redeemed **social condition**; to know even one life has **breathed easier** because you have lived. This is to have succeeded.

Once you have found your keywords, the next step is to create images out of them and place it on one of the systems that you have learned in this book. **Remember it is like your imagination is the pen and the system is the paper.** You can use a journey, your body, a car or anything that is already in your long-term memory. You can even link all the concepts together like you did with the presidents. Let me get you started; let's use a tree to remember the key concepts. Why a tree? Because it represents growth for me, and it is in your Long-term memory.

Imagine the roots **laughing** and **intelligent people** (you can imagine Einstein) are sitting at the base of the tree. Imagine **children** hugging the trunk of the tree (affection of children), and on the branches you can imagine **a nest (honest) full of critics.** You will notice that we have connected the first few key words to your system, and with a bit of repetition you will have it all in place.

If you choose, you can continue to connect the rest of the information to the leaves, thorns, and the fruit or to a park where the tree is planted. Once you have the key concepts then you need to read through the material a few times. The key words will make the text 'stickier' and your knowledge of English will help you to remember the syntax. Make the material come to life and you will remember more!

My friend, the late great Creighton Carvello, memorized Ernest Hemingway's novel *The Old Man and the Sea* and each word's numerical position. For example, you might have asked him the 6th word on Line 15 on Page 8 and he could name it. He did not use rote learning; he used a method similar to the one I have just shown you.

Like with anything in life it takes a bit of practice to be able to remember text with ease. When you master this, you will be able to remember any information that you need for your business or your life word-for-word. Actors have also successfully used this method to remember their lines. When you really know the information, you can feel and act it out more comfortably as well.

2. PRESENTING FROM MEMORY

"The human brain is a wonderful organ. It starts working as soon as you are born and doesn't stop until you get up to deliver a speech."

~ George Jessel

Do you enjoy watching a presentation where the presenter hides behind a piece of paper or a screen and reads all the information to you? No, you want to see a human being, making eye contact and communicating freely.

The purpose of any presentation is to get your audience to understand, believe and act on what you say. If you as a presenter can't remember your own content, how is your audience meant to remember it? If they can't remember it, they are not going to believe or act on it.

Many people are afraid of public speaking. I believe that the fear has a lot to do with the fear of forgetting information. Many people say, "I might hit a blank." The methods that you have already learned in this book will provide you with a solution. If you work with the methods you will never 'blank' out again.

I have been giving professional presentations for 15 years now and the last thing on my mind is the fear of forgetting information. When I present I use the memory strategies and the information is always there waiting for me to deliver it. I can also clearly remember jokes, slides, research, points that other people have said, and all my prepared content. I can loop back to any questions asked and be certain in my delivery. When you really remember the information, it builds confidence and you will look like you know what you are talking about. **Presentation power is memory power.**

You can eliminate the fear of forgetting by using memory methods like the journey, body, car, peg list, drawing your own pictures or making mind maps. Take charge and control of your content, because without notes you will look more professional in your delivery. When you present with the memory methods it is like you are reading from a teleprompter. You are not learning the information word-for-word but you are clearly remembering the structure.

If you don't move an audience you are not managing your content correctly. Great presenters know that audiences tend to remember the first and last bits of the presentation. Therefore they make their introduction and conclusion powerful and outstanding. They make their introductions more outstanding by opening with a memorable demonstration, question, fact, quote or a meaningful story. They also continually link information to the audience, making it more outstanding and keep repeating the main points. You can design your presentation with this FLOOR principle in mind. In a presentation we tend to remember:

F – First things

L – Last things

O – Outstanding information

O – Own links

R – Repeated information

If you use this principle you will get your audience to remember more – making your presentation more enjoyable.

If you have a clear structure installed in your head, it will be easier to move your audience, you will look more confident and you will be a much more powerful presenter.

3. ABSENT MINDS

"Is the object lost or are you lost?"

~ Anonymous

Have you ever had this experience, you are sitting in your room and you think, "I'm going to make chicken for dinner." You then walk to the kitchen and when you get there you think, "What am I doing here?" You may even open the refrigerator door, thinking the refrigerator will provide you with your answer. Or, have you ever parked your car and you can't find it when you get back? Have you ever wondered if you had taken your vitamins or other medication? And don't you just hate it when you put your car keys down and when you need them you can't find them?

If any of this has ever happened to you, then you are normal. Yes, normal! This all happens because familiarity breeds forgetfulness. All of our routines sometimes create a state of 'autopilot' and we often don't attend to what we are doing. The good news is that 95% of the time you are not absent minded. You remember where you put your car keys, you could find your car again, and you didn't put your pants in the fridge. Yet we 'beat' ourselves up for the mistakes we make 5% of the time. If you keep your focus on your absent minded moments you are going to create more absent mindedness. **Start to catch your memory doing things right and you will start to see improvements.**

It has been estimated that people squander forty days annually trying to remember things they've forgotten. People are becoming increasingly absent-minded as they struggle to cope with constant streams of information from mobile phones, the internet, radio, and television. With all our technology and systems in place we should be more at peace but we seem busier and more stressed than ever. As a result, we are regularly misplacing items or forgetting people's names.

We are living in an activity illusion and keeping our minds full of 'busyness' – no wonder we are absent minded. Making excuses for your absent mindedness doesn't solve anything.

So what is the solution? When you put items down, like your car keys, you need to bring yourself back to the present moment. Ask yourself questions like, "When am I going to use this next?" or say to yourself, "I am putting the keys on the table." Or, you could imagine that your keys are exploding the table. Try anything different to bring yourself back to the moment. Most things in life can be solved with more responsibility and awareness.

In Chapter 4, I talked about being all there. When you start to single task instead of trying to do a hundred things at once, then you will start to be more focused. Take action today! Clear the clutter. Get organized; think on paper. Bruce Sterling said, *"Chaos is the sexiest excuse for laziness ever invented."* Creating systems and using habitual places to put your items will save you massive amounts of time.

Do yourself a favor and stop trying to get attention for your absent mindedness. I hear you protesting, well why do you tell other people about these incidents if you didn't get attention for it? Decide today to rather bring yourself back to the power of now and pay more attention to the moment.

4. REMEMBERING PLAYING CARDS

Without a method the average person will only be able to remember about half a pack of cards in 30 minutes, if they are lucky. The average person doesn't have a way of trapping thoughts. So they are never really certain of what they know. With the method that I am about to teach you, you will be able to remember a shuffled pack in a few minutes. With the same method, I have been able to remember a pack in 45 seconds; with a bit of practice you will be able to do the same.

Remembering cards has many mental benefits. It is a great way to train your memory, it can help you in card games like Blackjack and Bridge, plus it has the added bonus of being a great demonstration of your memory power.

Knowing what you have already learned in this book, you now know that to remember something well you need to bring it to life. So how do you bring cards to life? First, we must create a picture for each card. Each card must have its own identity, so that you can distinguish it from the others and then place it on a long-term place or system. You can associate each card with a person that you know or you can make all the diamond cards celebrities, all the heart cards your family, spade cards people you work with, and the club cards your friends. That would be one way of organizing it.

With the system that I use, you will need to know the number code system from Chapter 12. The card system works in the same way as with numbers. Only this time, the first letter of each suite will start the name of each card e.g. the 3 of diamonds will be D for diamonds and 3 = M, add a vowel and you have DaM. All the Diamond cards will start with a D; all the hearts will start with H etc. And then you just add the converted number to the end of the card.

Here are all the images for all the suites:

Diamonds

A – Date (Ace is 1)

2 – Dan

3 – Dam

4 – Door

5 – Deal

6 – Dish

7 – Duck

8 – Dove

9 – Deep

10 – Dice (10 will be zero, s sound)

J – Diamond (Jacks will always be the image of the suite)

K – Ding (With Kings we use a word with 'ing' in it)

Q – Dean (With Queens we use a rhyming word)

Heart

A – Hat

2 – Hen

3 – Ham

4 – Hair

5 – Hail

6 – Hash (hash brown)

7 – Hack

8 – Hoof

9 – Hoop

10 – House

J – Heart (Jacks will always be the image of the suite)

K – Hinge (With Kings we use a word with 'ing' in it)

Q – Your queen of hearts (E.g. Princes Diana)

Spades

A – Sit

2 – Sun

3 – Sam (Uncle Sam)

4 – Sir

5 – Seal

6 – Sash

7 – Sack

8 – Safe

9 – Soap

10 – Seas

J – Spade (Jacks will always be the image of the suite)

K – Sing (With Kings we use a word with 'ing' in it)

Q – Steam (With Queens we use a rhyming word)

Clubs

A – Cat

2 – Can

3 – Camo (camouflage)

4 – Car

5 – Coal

6 – Cash

7 – Cake

8 – Cafe

9 – Cap

10 – Case

J – Club (Jacks will always be the image of the suite)

K – King (With Kings we use a word with 'ing' in it)

Q – Cream (With Queens we use a rhyming word)

Let's practice: imagine a **King** bashing down the **Door** and entering your **House**. He finds some **Ham** and **Duck** to eat in your fridge. With that silly story you remembered five cards – King of Clubs, 4 of Diamonds, 10 of Hearts, 3 of Hearts and 7 of Diamonds. Easy isn't it?

Once you have created images for each of the cards, you will have to get to know them. It will take a bit of time practising getting the card to automatically turn into the image, but with time it will become second nature.

To remember the whole shuffled pack you then create a journey of 52 places and you store each character on the journey, or you can link the cards together. These methods are not tricks; you are just using the memory fundamentals and therefore maximizing more of your memory potential.

This is memory gym, the more you work with it the more your overall memory will improve. It is a way to practise your memory skills. I know many people are not going to put in the effort to remember cards, but at least now you know how. This is just another example of how these methods can be applied to solve any memory problem.

5. STUDYING ANYTHING

*"Learning new information isn't helpful
unless it can be recalled later. Anything that
increases one's memory power increases
access to everything learned."*

~ Richard Restak, M.D.

There is no learning without memory. The more you can enhance your memory the better you will be able to learn. In every course there is some theory that needs to be remembered. The quicker you can get the theory down the more time you can spend on practising the information. Many of the first and second year University subjects are mostly memory based. If you have a strong memory system in place, you will succeed in anything that you choose to study.

There are a few things you should consider to enhance your performance in your area of study. First, never learn just to pass an exam. What is the purpose of doing well in an exam and not knowing what you have learned two weeks later? Learning is not a destination, it is a continuous process.

All the 'A' students that I have ever interviewed prepare and plan their learning. They do little bits over time and don't stress before the exam, because all the hard work has already been done. All the 'F' students overdose on energy drinks the night before and stress their way through the information hoping it will stick for the exam. So break your learning down and master the material over time.

Before you study anything make sure you have a strong PIC (Purpose, Interest and Curiosity) in mind. Review Chapter 4 to get more details on the PIC principle. Your vision will determine how much energy you will have for your learning and how hard you will be willing to work.

When studying it is also important to take breaks, as our mind can remain focused for only so long before we become unproductive and tense. When you return from a break you will feel refreshed and do more work in less time. Every 35 to 40 minutes take a break, take a walk and get away from whatever you're working on and give your mind a rest.

Get an overview and analyze the material that you have to cover. Mark out all the areas that you need to remember. In any subject the same concepts keep coming up, so make images for these key concepts and create an image 'vocabulary'. This is so that you don't have to keep on finding images for information that you have already created. Then create a memory system that will work for each section and store the information. Record your systems and go through them a few times to make sure you have all the content in your head. I have had students that have used one shopping centre to remember their entire syllabus. Using the methods, shared in this book, you will never have the experience of not being able to get information into your head again.

No matter what information you need to learn, these methods can be adapted so that you can find a solution and make the information 'sticky'. I have helped thousands of people to learn all kinds of material for school and university. I have helped medical students, law students, pilots, policeman, nurses, medical reps, miners, ornithologists, marketers and engineers. There isn't an area of study that won't benefit from these methods. These methods have no limits; the only limits are the excuses and judgments that you may place on them with your whining mind. Some people say, "I'm not creative and I don't make pictures", when I hear people say that to me, all I hear is, "I'm too lazy to put in the effort". If you choose to believe in limits you will live a limited life.

PART 3

CONTINUOUS USE

"Habits begin as offhanded remarks, ideas and images. And then, layer upon layer, through practice, they grow from cobwebs into cables that shackle or strengthen our lives."

~ Denis Waitley

CHAPTER 15

SELF-DISCIPLINE

*"We all love to win but how many people
love to train?"*

*~ Mark Spitz
(7 Gold medals in the1972 Olympics)*

There has never-ever been an undisciplined world champion. Our rewards are always directly proportional to our efforts. It sometimes takes years of training to develop abilities in the area in which we would like to achieve success. People say, "That person has such a talent," but they never look down the road to see how many hours have been spent training. If you want to master the skills that you have learned in this book, or if you want to master anything, you need self-discipline.

Self-discipline is not self-deprivation. It is about raising your standards and going for and being more.

Many people think that things are going to magically appear in their lives. Think about it... people want beautiful healthy teeth, but they don't have the self-discipline to floss them. Is it expensive? Does it take a lot of time? Is it difficult to do? It is none of these. How can they expect to change any area of their lives if they can't even bring themselves to do that? So why don't people floss?

I once read an article on *CNN.com* that stated, "Up to 59% of Glaucoma patients regularly skip their eye drops, even though untreated glaucoma can lead to blindness." If you have glaucoma you are going to lose your eyesight if you don't use your drops! Why don't people do it?

People simply don't do it because they think that the future will be a better place than today, without doing anything to make it better.

What do you want? What are you doing daily? If your daily actions are not moving you in the direction of what you want, then you will never get what you want. Common sense, isn't it?

It is not that your goals are physically impossible; it is more that you lack the self-discipline to stick to them. There are four keys to creating more self-discipline in your life and the first one is:

1. CREATE A VISION

Your inner vision and your energy are connected. If you wake up in the morning and focus on all the bad things that could possibly happen in a day, your energy level will be low. If you wake up and imagine all the exciting possibilities, and focus on all the great things that you get to do, your energy level lifts. Where your attention goes, your energy flows.

David Campbell said, *"Discipline is remembering what you want."* The more reasons you have to do something the better your inner movie will be, and therefore the more energy you will create to do it. If your excuses are high and your reasons are low, you will have no discipline to start. If your reasons are high and your excuses are low, you will have lots of motives, and motives in action creates motivation. Always ask yourself, "How badly do I want it?" If you really, really want it, you will create a strong vision and you will have the self-discipline to do it.

2. MAKE A DECISION

All change happens only when you make a true decision to change. When you make a true decision you will not allow for any other possibility. Make a commitment to yourself that this is the way that you are going to live your life.

For anything to happen in your life you have to schedule it. Decide to make it part of your routine.

3. STOP LISTENING TO YOUR FEELINGS

Elbert Hubbard said, *"Self-discipline is the ability to make yourself do what you should do, when you should do it, whether you feel like it or not."* When people want to start a task that they have to complete and say something like, "I will do this tomorrow" a loop closes in their mind and they are happy to continue without doing it... because they will do it tomorrow. The problem is that when tomorrow comes the same loop just repeats itself. Or if you say, "I just don't feel like it" a loop closes because you have tricked yourself into thinking that you will do it when you do feel like it. These pictures and voices, that we control, create our feelings. If you want emotional mastery learn to take control of these pictures, movies, and voices that you run in your mind.

Some people say, "I have to listen to my inner voice because it guides my intuition." Listen to your intuition or feelings when you are deciding to pass a truck on a busy road, making a massive decision or whether you should climb into an elevator with a freaky looking guy. But when you are following a discipline these feelings only get in the way. If you have to floss your teeth, you don't have to consult your intuition, you just do it. When you have to exercise you don't have to listen to your feelings, just do it. William James said, *"The more we struggle and debate, the more we reconsider and delay, the less likely we are to act."*

Schedule a time in the day for memory training and practise – whether you feel like it or not.

4. DAILY ACTION

If you want to develop a habit then the only way to achieve this is by doing something daily. You have to review your new skill to renew it. Only by consistently practising your discipline can you turn it into a skill. Most of the research that I have read says it takes 21 days to develop a new habit. In my experience it takes a lot longer. Some people think that once the 21 days are up the brain will then take over. Then after twenty-one days they give up, waiting for their brain to do the rest. Self-discipline requires you to make a decision daily. Self-discipline requires you to start fresh every day. Every day is a new day. You don't have to practise this skill for the rest of your life. Just for today.

I believe that life does not reward idleness. If you put your arm in a sling for a week you start to lose the use of many of your major muscles. Your brain is made of flesh and blood like the rest of your body, so if you use it, it will improve and if you don't you will lose it. **The only way you get good at anything is through self-discipline; remember life only rewards action!**

CHAPTER 16

REVIEW TO RENEW

*"You know as well as I do that it is entirely
wrong to assume that any subject matter
which we once learned and mastered will
remain our mental property forever."*

~ Bruno Furst

It has been estimated that two years after leaving school, the average person only remembers three weeks' worth of lessons.

Think about it in your own life. Do you still remember all those theorems? That means that after 12 years all you have left is three weeks. The average person that passes a test today would never pass that same test four weeks later. Final exams are really final!

In Spitzer's experiment it was found that the average person who learns textbook material (without memory methods) remembers only the following:

After 1 day: 54%

After 7 days: 35%

After 14 days: 21%

After 21 days: 19%

After 28 days: 18%

The above shows that the average student only remembers 18% of their work after a 28-day holiday. That means the lecturer or trainer only has 18% of the knowledge to build new knowledge onto. The average company or student loses 82% of the information or 82 cents out of every training dollar after 28 days. Any training is a waste of time if there is not a process of review!

Many people feel that they can never forget the information that they learned using the memory methods and systems. The memory methods make the learning process fun and more effective. They create such a strong impression and it is so different to your mind that you have to remember it, and consequently it sticks. The methods help to store the memory quickly for a medium term, but to make sure that the information remains in your mind you need to review and recite it.

The reason we review is to make the information more solid in our minds. The only way we can build on a memory is if we can remember it. Your memory is like a bank: the more you put into it the more it grows. Review also helps you to create more long-term memories.

Repetition or rote learning on its own (without the methods) is no fun; it takes long and can often result in an aversion to learning. Memorizing should be a pleasure; it should be more like a game.

Reviewing when using the memory methods doesn't require a lot of time. It is just a process of thinking about it, and making sure that the pictures are strong and that you can clearly see them. Then recite any information that you want to stick in your mind.

I have found that if you review your information in a specified time frame you increase recall. If you repeat it after ten minutes of learning the information it will remain in your memory for at least an hour. The first review should always be done backwards. Reviewing images backwards helps you to remember them more effectively.

If you learn concepts in reverse you create a new impression in your mind and this makes information more outstanding. It just seems to make the memory so much stronger. Once you have done this, you review at longer and longer intervals: **review after 1 hour then 1 day, 3 days, 7 days, 14 days, 21 days, 28 days, 2 months, 3 months and then it should be in your**

memory forever. During the first 72-hour period the knowledge transfers into a deeper stronger memory. So if you are using a route or journey system, after the first 72-hours you will be able to reuse the journey for new information. However, if you have information that you want to keep forever, rather assign it its own route or system and review it often.

Review takes discipline, but it keeps information fresh in your mind. It keeps it alive. It keeps it awake so that you can connect more information to that existing information. The more that you connect to that information the stronger the information becomes. Your mind is the only computer in the world with this characteristic: the more you put into it, the more it will hold.

The perfect way to learn is to make lots of firsts and lasts by having lots of breaks, make your information outstanding, make your own links (using memory methods) and then you review it to keep it ready in your mind for new learning.

No matter how many times you memorize something, you will have to start over from the beginning if you let yourself forget it. You have to spread out your revision over longer and longer periods of time. If you use it you will strengthen the information, and you will remember it.

When you review, it helps you to think more about what you are remembering. By thinking about it you begin to really understand it too. It is important to use this information when remembering names. Only if you review them are you going to remember them. If you use the information often it acts as a review. You either use it, or you lose it from your instant recall.

You should **always use the power of review to put a lid on your learning to prevent your learning from escaping**.

We have learned that the only way that you improve is to get rid of anything that is **preventing** you from improving. So we got rid of the blocks to your mind like excuses, limiting beliefs and learning to single task, and then we became more **willing** to learn more. Then we learned **how** to improve through the SEE principle of imagination. We have learned the different memory methods – the link story method, memory art, the body and car method, the route or journey method, the peg systems, the number code, and remembering names. These methods are only limited by your own imagination and level of self-discipline. We now also know how to review.

Remember to review to renew.

ENDINGS ARE THE SEEDS
FOR BEGINNINGS

"If you're hoping to harvest a life of great deeds, remember you first have to plant some great seeds."

~ Denis Waitley

You are the source of all your memories and **remembering is a choice!** There is no magic when it comes to memory improvement; there is only management.

Memory skills are an important tool in your self-improvement arsenal. I have given you many tools, but remember **batteries are not included**. You need to provide the energy to make it work. The information you have received will change your life for the better... use it! Memory training will enable you to create more certainty with information. Certainty fosters confidence, and will give you a glimpse of your amazing ability.

Brice Marden said: *"The possibilities of thought training are infinite, its consequences eternal, and yet few take the pains to direct their thinking into channels that will do them good, but instead leave all to chance."*

Today you have two choices. You can take the **first** option: you can leave it all to chance and do what you have always done, but you will get what you have always gotten. Or, you can take the pains and decide today to take the **second** option: do different to become different. Take these tools, make them your own, practise hard, and unleash the power of your memory.

"May you never forget what is worth remembering, nor ever remember what is best forgotten."

~ Irish Blessing

BIBLIOGRAPHY

1. Buzan, T. 1995. *Use Your Memory*. London: BBC books.

2. Buzan, T. 1995. *Use Your Head*. London: BBC books.

3. Buzan, T. 2001. *Head First*. London: Thorsons.

4. Baddeley, A, Eysenck, M.W, Anderson, M.C. 2009. *Memory*. USA: Psychology Press.

5. Covey, S. 1989. *The Seven Habits of Highly Effective People: Powerful Lessons in Personal Change*. Britain: Simon & Schuster Ltd.

6. Lorayne, H. 1992. *Improve Exam Results In 30 days*. London: Thorsons.

7. Luria, A.R. 1998. *The Mind of the Mnemonist*. London: Harvard University Press.

8. Maxwell, J.C. 2004. *Today Matters: 12 Daily Practices to Guarantee Tomorrow's Success*. USA: Time Warner Book Group.

9. Robbins, A. 1992. *Awaken The Giant Within*. London. Simon & Schuster Ltd.

10. Worthen, J and Reed Hunt, R. 2011. *Mnemonology: Mnemonics for the 21st Century*. USA: Psychology Press.

11. Medina, J. 2008. *Brain Rules: 12 Principles for Surviving and Thriving at Work, Home, and School*. USA: Pear Press.

12. Lorayne, H. 1957. *How To Develop A Superpower Memory*. New York: Frederick Fell.

13. Higbee, K. 2001. *Your Memory : How It Works and How to Improve It.* Da Capo Press; 2nd edition

14. Price, I. 2011. *The Activity Illusion*. Matador

15. Katie, B. 2008. *Loving What Is: How Four Questions Can Change Your Life*. Ebury Digital

16. Hall, M. 2013. *Movie Mind*. USA: L. Michael Hall

17. Demartini, J. 2008. The Riches within: your seven secret treasures. USA: Hay House, INC.

18. Gruneberg, M. 1987. *Linkword Language System – Italian*. UK: Corgi Books

19. Furst, B. 1949. *Stop Forgetting.*USA: Greenberg.

20. Kandel, E.R. 2007. *In Search of Memory: The Emergence of New Science of Mind.* USA: W.W.Norton & Company.

21. Drawings done by Jac Hamman.

22. Royalty-free images from ***www.pixabay.com***. Graphics created by Michelle Revolta.

ABOUT THE AUTHOR

For over 25 years, **KEVIN HORSLEY** has been analyzing the mind and memory and its capacity for brilliance. He is one of only a few people in the world to have received the title *International Grandmaster of Memory*.

He is a World Memory Championship medalist, and a two-time World Record holder for *The Everest of Memory Tests*. Kevin is also an author of four books, and the designer of a times table game with the Serious Games Institute at North-West University Vaal Campus.

Kevin is an International professional speaker, and assists organizations in improving their learning, motivation, creativity, and thinking.

Learn more about Kevin at ***www.supermemory.co.za***

INDEX

ONE LAST THING...

If you enjoyed this book or found it useful I'd be very grateful if you'd post a short review on Amazon. Your support really does make a difference and I read all the reviews personally so I can get your feedback and make this book even better.

If you'd like to leave a review then all you need to do is go to the following URL of this book's page on Amazon here: *http://amzn.to/Mt45dT*

Thanks again for your support!

Name:
FLIGHT PITTS -ATL -WPB
Conf# GXFMX8
1-800-221-12-12
Delta
Conf #

Conf# GXFMX8

48505144R00106

Made in the USA
San Bernardino, CA
27 April 2017